From
Toy Boys
To
Shed Men

This is a two decade journey starting out as Kim's Toyboys to the name it is today, Mandurah Men's Shed.

From
Toy Boys
To
Shed Men

KEVIN J. ATKINS

CONSCIOUS CARE PUBLISHING

FROM TOY BOYS TO SHED MEN

Copyright © 2021 by Kevin J. Atkins. All rights reserved.

First Published 2021 by: Conscious Care Publishing
PO Box 776, Rockingham, WA 6968, Australia
www.consciouscarepublishing.com

First Edition printed April 2021.

Notice of Rights
This book is sold subject to the condition that it shall not, by way of trade or otherwise, be lent, resold, hired out, or otherwise circulated without the publisher's prior consent, in any form of binding or cover, other than that in which it is published, and without a similar condition, including this condition being imposed on the subsequent purchaser. All rights reserved by the publisher. No part of this publication may be reproduced, stored in a retrieval system, or transmitted in any form, or by any means, electronic, digital, mechanical, photocopying, scanning, recorded or otherwise, without the prior written permission of the copyright owner. Requests to the copyright owner should be addressed to Permissions Department, Conscious Care Publishing, PO Box 776, Rockingham, WA 6968, Australia, email: admin@consciouscarepublishing.com

Limits of Liability/Disclaimer of Warranty:
While the publisher and author have used their best efforts in preparing this book, they make no representations or warranties with respect to the accuracy or completeness of the contents of this book and specifically disclaim any implied warranties of merchantability or fitness for a particular purpose. No warranty may be created or extended by sales representatives or written sales materials. The advice and strategies contained herein may not be suitable for your situation. You should consult with a professional where appropriate. The intent of the author is only to offer information for a general nature. Neither the publisher nor author shall be liable for any loss of profit or any other commercial damages, including but not limited to special, incidental, consequential, or other damages. The author and the publisher assume no responsibility for your actions.

Where photographic images have been provided by the author and people are depicted, such images are being used for illustrative purposes only. Product names may be trademarks or registered trademarks, and are used for identification and explanation without intent to infringe. Conscious Care Publishing publishes in a variety of print and electronic format and by print-on-demand. Some material included with standard print versions of this book may not be included in e-books or in print-on-demand. If this book refers to media such as a CD or DVD that is not included in the version you purchased, you may download this material at www.conscious-carepublishing.com

National Library of Australia Cataloguing-in-Publication entry:
Author: Atkins, Kevin 1942-
From Toy Boys to Shed Men / by Kevin Atkins
ISBN 9780645089226 (Paperback)

Printed by Lightning Source
Typeset & cover design by Conscious Care Publishing

ISBN: 978-0-6450892-2-6

ACKNOWLEDGEMENTS

I would like to thank the following people as they were instrumental in helping me to complete this journey;

Paul Ellis, for being a good record keeper and providing me with invaluable reference material.

Graeme Gordon, for being able to fill in the gaps when records were a bit sketchy.

John and Irene Boulton, for having elephantine memories that gave me so much background information and anecdotal stories.

**Dedicated to the memory Kim Butcher,
who started the ball rolling**

INTRODUCTION

It is a Tuesday morning in August 2019 and a group of retired old farts are having their morning break from wood projects at the Mandurah Men's Shed. As usual the discussion revolves around how they can solve the world's problems, where their next caravan trip will be and how many pills they have to take each day.

Then, someone mentioned the name of a Shed member who no longer attends, and the odd things that person used to get up to. That reminded other guys of past antics people carried out, stories about what others did and the activities the shed had achieved.

It dawned on me at that stage that what was being talked about here was part of the history of Mandurah and the culture of a segment of retirees. There are often discussions like this, particularly from the time when the operation was called Kim's Toyboys. That era has a special place in the hearts of the original members. What we need to do is get a record of this before too many of our members go to that big shed in the sky.

The question then was "Who do we get to chronicle this?" Looking at who we currently had as members I couldn't see too many candidates who might fit the bill or even volunteer. The problem was that almost all of the members came from a manual working type of background and were not used to writing tasks. I kept telling myself "Kev, you have enough on your plate let someone else take it on". I had a fierce tussle with my conscience but in the end the devil won out and here I am putting pen to paper.

Where to start?

Firstly, let me say this is not my story. I am just the scribe. I do feature later on in the story but it is mainly in my capacity as the secretary/treasurer. This is about the development of a woodworking team, their stories and how they have built a formidable presence. It is the trials and tribulations, the good and bad times, the anecdotes and how a talented bunch of old guys developed a wonderful operation.

I am going to rely heavily on the longstanding members as some of them have been around since day one. The shed has grown somewhat over the last twenty years and has not only seen a change in direction but has had to come to grips with increasing Government regulations. I hope others will be able to add information that paints a total picture of the journey.

I expect there will be many hours of interviews and discussions as indications are there are many stories to be told. I am a relative newcomer to the shed so will have to rely on the support of others to fill in the blanks for me.

Don't be fooled by the flow of words so far. I am sweating bullets worrying whether I can pull it all together in some sort of sensible format. Writing something like this is totally new to me, so fingers crossed that the end product will be interesting and enjoyable.

Since my first thoughts, I have spent many sleepless hours stressing as to how I could put it all together. What will the format be? Who will I be able to talk to? Will the members be supportive? Am I just procrastinating? In the end the decision was to just jump in feet first and get the job done. To put together this story is my way of saying thank you for the enjoyment the shed has brought to me

It is now November 2019 and I figure it will take some time to investigate and compile the whole kit and caboodle. I am not a "wordy" type of person so the descriptions may be short and to the point.

No more rabbiting on, so sit back and enjoy the journey of:

"From Toy Boys to Shed Men".

Kevin J Atkins

CONTENTS

IN THE BEGINNING	**1**
CHAPTER 1	2
YEAR 1994	**4**
CHAPTER 2	5
YEAR 2000	**8**
CHAPTER 3	9
YEAR 2001	**12**
CHAPTER 4	13
CHAPTER 5	16
CHAPTER 6	18
YEAR 2002	**24**
CHAPTER 7	25
YEAR 2003	**29**
CHAPTER 8	30
CHAPTER 9	32
YEAR 2004	**38**
CHAPTER 10	39
CHAPTER 11	40
YEAR 2005	**43**
CHAPTER 12	44
CHAPTER 13	45
YEAR 2006	**49**
CHAPTER 14	50
YEAR 2007	**53**
CHAPTER 15	54
CHAPTER 16	55
YEAR 2008	**59**
CHAPTER 17	60
YEAR 2009	**63**
CHAPTER 18	64

CHAPTER 19	65
YEAR 2010	**70**
CHAPTER 20	71
YEAR 2011	**73**
CHAPTER 21	74
CHAPTER 22	76
YEAR 2012	**79**
CHAPTER 23	80
CHAPTER 24	81
YEAR 2013	**86**
CHAPTER 25	87
CHAPTER 26	90
YEAR 2014	**94**
CHAPTER 27	95
CHAPTER 28	97
YEAR 2015	**101**
CHAPTER 29	102
CHAPTER 30	103
YEAR 2016	**107**
CHAPTER 31	108
CHAPTER 32	113
YEAR 2017	**117**
CHAPTER 33	118
CHAPTER 34	119
YEAR 2018	**121**
CHAPTER 35	122
CHAPTER 36	126
YEAR 2019	**131**
CHAPTER 37	132
CHAPTER 38	137
YEAR 2020	**144**
CHAPTER 39	145
CHAPTER 40	147
CHAPTER 41	151
CHAPTER 42	153
CHAPTER 43	160
JOURNEY'S END	**166**
THE AUTHOR	**169**

IN THE BEGINNING

CHAPTER 1

It is fair to say that **Kim Butcher** was the father of the Men's Shed. Because of this I would like to spend some time looking at his background and what brought him to develop Kim's Toyboys.

It wasn't widely known, but Kim's real name is Clifton Harold Butcher. He was called Kim as a youngster and it stuck throughout his life.

Being brought up on a farm in Bruce Rock, and then later running it, Kim became adept at repairing machinery, particularly in the welding aspects. He was quick to say;

"I am petty handy with a welder, but hopeless at joining two pieces of wood together".

This is an interesting statement bearing in mind what he was able to achieve later in life. Farming didn't work out so he and his wife Betty bought some school buses and ran that service in and around Bruce Rock for about 14 years.

Finally they sold up in Bruce Rock and moved to the "big smoke". They lived in the Perth suburb of Bedford, but had bought a house in Riverview, Coodanup which they used as a holiday place. Kim did a variety of jobs. Delivering telegrams, driving a delivery truck for Sadleir's, handyman for a metal company, general dogsbody for Perth City Council. (You will note that there is still nothing to do with woodworking).

After eight years that was it - they had had enough of city living. They up sticks and moved into their house in Riverview. Feeling much better, Kim set about getting a job. He applied for, and got, a job as a postman with the Mandurah Post Office.

He happily did that for the next eight years until the Post Office decided to part company with him in 1992. (Still no woodworking).

At that stage Kim said to Betty;

"I think we should go on a trip round Australia".

IN THE BEGINNING

So, Betty also quit her job at the Post Office and off they went in an old ute and caravan. This kept them busy for the next two years.

Trolley

• MANDURAH postman, Kim Butcher has traded in his bicycle for "shank's pony" and this lightweight, collapsible Australia Post trolley.

Mr Butcher says the trolley is more efficient and allows him to give his customers personal service.

He has become a familiar figure in the central Mandurah business district, and now has time for a chat with his customers as he delivers their mail.

Australia Post uses the trolleys in the central Perth business district but Mandurah's postman is the first in a country area to be issued with one.

Postie Kim on the job

YEAR 1994

CHAPTER 2

It was now 1994 and the Butchers moved to Mandurah as their permanent home. This was the start of Kim's retirement and his big decision was:

"What am I going to do now?"

"I started doing gardening and odd jobs for elderly people, but then thought if I can't look after my own garden, I'm not going to look after someone else's." Kim said.

He never particularly liked woodwork and preferred working with steel. But his hands got bruised and battered working with steel so he changed to woodwork.

Needing somewhere to work properly, he built a shed on their property. Not just any old shed, but one with plenty of room. The final result was 6 metres by 8 metres with a mezzanine section for storage.

Kim's comment was "That should be big enough and keep me going for while". Little did he realise how that statement would prove to be wrong.

Over the next few years he gradually built up the various tools and machines needed to do the work. He read a countless number of books on woodworking procedures and bit by bit built up his skills. Despite his earlier comment that he couldn't join two pieces of wood together, he took to it like a duck to water.

Betty's brother, Don Gunn, was a cabinet maker and was a big help in developing Kim's woodworking skills. His earlier attempts were basic but as time went on he became a very accomplished woodworker. He was a very patient person and this helped him to stick to the task until he could produce toys that were second to none.

Kim in his original shed

He met a fellow named **Bill Bowen**, who was a cabinet maker, and did some community work with children. They became good friends and Bill was also instrumental in teaching Kim woodworking skills. They both liked the idea of helping underprivileged kids so decided that making wooden toys would be the go. Bill became a valuable member of the Toyboys until he hung up his hammer and saw in 2005.

They started slowly, making a few toys which they gave to community groups. Over time the need by underprivileged families and community groups increased, so they could see that just working on their own was not going to meet the demand. This started the thought process going as to how they could meet that demand.

In 1998 Kim was also doing some volunteer work with Support Our Seniors (SOS) and met **Bob Loftus**. Neither of them were happy with the operations at SOS so Kim said to Bob "Why don't we quit this and you come with me to my shed where we will concentrate on making children's toys".

This sounded good to Bob, except that he knew how to use a hammer and that was the extent of his woodworking skills. He was a butcher (occupation, not a Kim relative) prior to retiring and was lacking in manual work experience.

YEAR 1994

Kim took him under his wing and taught him the art of making wooden toys. He gradually progressed and ended up quite adept in turning out toys.

When asked how he remembers the Toyboys he said "They were a happy bunch of old guys who worked in for a common goal that put a smile on kid's faces".

Bob moved to Fremantle in 2003 and as it was now too far to travel twice weekly Mandurah he said farewell to the Toyboys.

Kim's confidence in making toys was growing. His nephew worked for a cement mixing company and Kim thought it might be a good idea if he could make a model cement mixer for him. With determination he slowly and surely plodded away until he had a model that was as good as the best of them could produce. This is just one example of that strong character.

Kim was very proud of this.

YEAR 2000

CHAPTER 3

Kim's idea was that he could set up a volunteer group of likeminded people who could produce more toys to help meet the demand. It was felt that retirees would be an ideal target area to recruit people.

His thoughts were that there were people who were no longer working, had some time their hands and maybe needed a bit of camaraderie external to the family home. They probably had prior woodworking skills or even had their own workshops.

Through the Peel Volunteer Centre, Kim arranged for a newspaper article inviting people "with experience in making toys, or willing to learn" to contact the "Old Toyboys Group".

Volunteer toymaker sought

PEEL Volunteer Centre's Position of the Month is as a toymaker/carpenter with the Retired and Senior Volunteer Program's Old Toyboys Group.

The position involves making and repairing wooden toys for children and repairing bicycles.

RSVP's Old Toyboys Group are looking for someone who enjoys working within a group with experience in making wooden toys, or is willing to learn.

Seniors and/or retired people are welcome.

The group's objective is to create an environment that is in partnership with the community to provide handmade toys that will be distributed to needy families.

The organisation also caters for the interests and needs of children and donates toys to be used in raffles for fundraising.

For more information contact 9581 1187.

The first to respond was **Paul Ellis**. Paul had worked for Homeswest as a carpenter for a number of years but when they decided to use contractors he was cast aside. He went through the process of becoming a "certified" volunteer and started looking at community work. He was doing some gardening and yard work for pensioners, but as with Kim, it was just not his thing.

When he saw the article in the paper he couldn't wait to contact Kim and join the woodworking group. Paul had his own workshop and was experienced in making wooden models cars, boats, trucks, racers, you name it, and he produced some really amazing pieces.

Paul with two of his models

Paul's forte became making dolls houses and over the years has produced some stunning pieces. He is the only one remaining, from the original Toyboys, still turning out toys with the Mandurah Men's Shed.

Brenton (Brent) Taylor came along a short time later. Having retired from Telstra he started community work in the Mandurah Area. While doing volunteer work walking dogs for Community Canines he heard about Kim's Toyboys. As he "dabbled" a bit in backyard woodworking he thought this might be for him.

So off he went and spoke to Kim about joining. It turned out to be a good move by him as he enjoyed the making of toys. Brent also became the "wood scrounger". He took upon himself to call on building sites and snaffle any spare timber that was "surplus to requirements".

"During my time with Kim's Toyboys I don't think there was a building site I did not visit" said Brent.

Brent fondly remembers the years that he spent there and finally went into full retirement in 2011.

Another early Toyboy was **David Brown.** David married Perth girl Ruth in 1976 but then went back to the UK to work. He was made redundant as a gas engineer in 1996 so they moved back permanently to WA.

He saw the article in the paper and approached Kim about joining. The only problem was, he was allergic to fine wood dust which was a drawback if he was to make toys. It turned out however that David knew bicycles so they decided they would collect bicycles no longer wanted by people and "recycle" them (no pun intended).

It was in 2004 that the source of bicycles started to dry up and buying parts was not financially viable. Accordingly, they had to let this part of the operation go. As both his and Ruth's parents now needed full time care it was an opportune time to say goodbye to the Toyboys.

Robert Durrant joined the group briefly, but obtained a full time job and left.

With the growing number of men on a waiting list to join, working space in Kim's shed was getting too cramped to accommodate many more. Feelers were put out to see if they could obtain better premises.

An approach was made to the Mandurah City Council through David Templeman MLA to see if they had any suitable premises available. The result was an empty double garage between the Senior Citizens Association and a Day Care Centre in Ormsby Terrace. While not perfect, it did provide extra space to what they currently had.

So, a convoy of cars, trucks and trailers was organized to cart machinery and tools from Kim's shed to the new premises.. Some work and storage was still done at Kim's place so the teams became split.

While they were grateful to have these premises, problems were starting to emerge. The front was just roller doors so anybody could stroll in. The concern was that children from the Day Care Centre could wander in.

They only had the use of it two days a week and on the other days other people had access. This caused security problems with their machinery and gear. As there were no dust extraction units, the concern was that member's health could be affected. Once more they kept an eye out for premises that might be better.

YEAR 2001

CHAPTER 4

There was now a growing group producing a steady supply of toys. But, to prosper they could not rely on their own resources. As a bunch of retirees/pensioners, funds can only stretch so far.

Some of the boys.
L to R David Brown, Alec Osbourne, Paul Ellis, Bob Loftus,
Bill Bowen, Brenton Taylor.
Lying down on the job – Kim Butcher

FROM TOY BOYS TO SHED MEN

It was agreed that they should become a formal group, operation or whatever you might call them, as this would help when seeking financial assistance from various quarters. On went the thinking caps.

Firstly, the group decided that Kim's name should be in there to recognise the determination to form a group and the generosity of having his shed and machinery as the work place.

"What do we do? We make toys". It was obvious therefore that "toys" should be in there somewhere.

They liked the idea of calling themselves "boys" as they were young at heart and liked hanging around in a "gang". Plus, Kim had loosely tagged them the Old ToyBoys Group.

Further discussion failed to bring up anything else that epitomised what they were. So, it was decided to work with the above.

It didn't take long for agreement to be reached and *"Kim's Toyboys"* was born.

Kim's vision of a cohesive community minded group was coming to fruition. The members would probably be:

- √ Over the age of 55 (but not compulsory).
- √ No longer working for a boss (wife or partner excepted).
- √ Be community minded,
- √ Will enjoy the camaraderie of a "work place".
- √ Help train those with lesser skills.
- √ Be able to socialise from time to time.
- √ Will share ideas, plans and techniques.
- √ Have a high work standard in making toys.

It was considered that the advantages of being a Toyboy were: "

"*that of being both a helper and the helped*".

A new era in community work had begun.

It would be remiss of me not to acknowledge the great support that **David Templeman MLA** has given us over the years.

He first got to know Kim and Betty in late 1998 while he was the Deputy Mayor of Mandurah. He had heard from friends that there was a fellow making wooden toys so he looked him up.

"Kim and Betty really became friends before any dealings with the group in an official capacity" said David.

David could see that the boys were working in relatively cramped quarters, so kept one eye out for any chance of getting a decent building for them. I didn't take long, and he was able to help secure them the new premises in Ormsby Terrace.

Shortly after that David was made an Honorary Toyboy. We are still waiting for him to come in one day and churn out a few toys. Though I must admit he has popped in a few times and provided morning tea.

He has stayed in touch with the group over the years and given his support whenever he could. That support really came to the fore in 2012 when the boys needed to move from Community First and had nowhere to go. That support resulted in the Toyboys being housed at what is now John Tonkin College.

David is still our Patron and a great advocate of our operation because of the support we give to community groups and underprivileged kids by providing wooden toys.

CHAPTER 5

The first official meeting of Kim's Toyboys took place on 5th April 2001.

The elected office holders were:

> President – Kim Butcher.
> Vice-President – Bob Loftus
> Treasurer - Bob Durrant
> Acting Secretary – David brown

There was to be no "committee" as all members were able to attend meetings and have input.

The others in attendance were:

> Paul Ellis
> Brenton Taylor
> Alec Osbourne
> Bill Bowen

To add credence to the operation it was decided to register as an incorporated body. It was felt that should the group need to seek grants or sponsoring from businesses it would auger well to be a registered body.

The registration was completed on 4th July 2001, so henceforth they were officially known as Kim's Toyboys Inc.

The objects of The Association (Kim's Toyboys Inc.) were set as:

1. "For volunteers to meet regularly, make wooden toys, repair bicycles, skates, skate boards and other toys for use by under-privileged children.

2. From time to time undertake activities to raise funds for the purpose of purchasing goods and equipment to make and repair toys and bicycles."

A few months later Bob Durrant obtained a full time job, so Paul Ellis became Acting Treasurer until the next Annual General Meeting was held.

CHAPTER 6

So began operations under the new flag.

It was decided that the distinctive toy train should appear where possible on printed matter to typify what the Toyboys were about.

Family and Children's Services (FCS) were generous in granting funds of $2,000 towards the purchase of additional machinery and tools. With a smile on their faces, off the boys went to Bunnings to fill up their trollies.

FCS was very supportive of the Toyboys over the following years. Mark and Sue Perkins from FCS attended many of their meetings and lent a hand when necessary. At a later stage the FCS premises were used to hold Toyboy meetings. In July Sue Taylor took on the role of minute taker at meetings.

The working days were set down as Tuesday and Thursday between the hours of 9.00am and 3.00pm. There was no mandatory attendance and members could attend as it suited them. Most of them had their own workshops and made items at home.

As you can appreciate, running any sort of business or "operation" takes money and

YEAR 2001

the Toyboys were no different. For them there were machinery repairs, tool replacements, glue, screws, sandpaper and a whole lot of woodworking bits and pieces. They relied as much as possible on having timber donated but there were still times when they had to buy some. There were overheads such as electricity, insurance and registration fees. So, like all of us they had to meet the bills somehow.

They never actively promoted the sale of their toys but as their reputation grew people would approach them to buy a particular toy they had made. A small charge may be made, but more often than not a bigger voluntary donation would be given. Some of the community groups that they donated toys to would sometimes give a small donation to show their appreciation.

This was fine to a point, but it was felt that their coffers should be built up to cater for unforeseen snags that may arise. So, it was decided that the old favourite "The Raffle" would be the way to go. This was their first effort into raffle funding, but It wasn't hard to decide what the prizes would be – Wooden Toys. It was agreed that the prizes would be:

    First Prize – Elizabethan Dolls House
    Second Prize – Childs Table and 4 Chairs
    Third Prize – Childs Truck & Trailer

The raffle prizes

It was June now and the raffle was to be held in December. This allowed plenty of time for the production of the prizes, so the boys got to work. As you can see on the previous page, the final result was impressive.

This was when Bob Loftus put his hand up. "I may not be the best toymaker, but I have the gift of the gab so I'll work shopping centres selling tickets" he said.

All the boys were put to work selling the raffle tickets. It was not just their personal contacts that were to be targeted. Space was booked at shopping centres and a roster set up for the gang to target shoppers. It was relatively successful with a net profit made of $1,845 (bearing in mind tickets were only $1 each).

Despite financial pressures the boys still managed to churn out a considerable number of toys. There were a growing number of men wanting to join and working conditions at Ormsby Terrace were not ideal. Feelers were put out to see if they could obtain better premises.

The year saw them provide toys for:

> Foodbank for inclusion in Xmas hampers for needy families.
> Friends of Peel Hospital.
> Women's Refuge Centre.
> Family and Children's Services for delivery to underprivileged children and Church groups.

Christmas is not always a joyful time for some families as their financial position is not strong. If there are children in the family it is them who may miss out on having Santa Claus visit them.

Kim's Toyboys came partly to the rescue!

They made and stockpiled wooden toys during the year so they can distribute them to needy families through welfare services and community groups. Unfortunately they could not help everybody, but they certainly put a smile on a lot of kid's faces.

YEAR 2001

Toy makers chip in

Hundreds of toys have been made by Kim's Toy Boys for Christmas. Picture: LINDA BOLT

MANDURAH children will have an extra big smile on their faces this Christmas thanks to the generosity of a volunteer group.

Kim's Toy Boys, made up of 10 retirees, have made hundreds of wooden toys over the past six months to be included in the Christmas food hamper made up by welfare authorities.

Despite not all being former carpenters, the group has worked in the Margaret Harris Day Centre workshop two half-days a week, making toys out of wood donated by local businesses.

The template for each toy has been checked and approved by the Ministry of Consumer Protection, as has the glue being used, to ensure their suitability for children.

The toys range from trucks to trains, planes, dolls chairs and even an abacus.

Kim Butcher, who started the group about two years ago, said there were not as many wooden toys around for children these days.

Wives of the Toy Boys had also helped out by making things such as knitted bears to hand out.

Family and Children's Services financial resources manager Mark Perkins said the hampers would be distributed to needy families just before Christmas.

FROM TOY BOYS TO SHED MEN

Peter Addison -   Joined in September 2001 and left in October 2002.

He was a builder in Geraldton for many years before finishing has working life with the local council. The northern heat had finally got to him so he moved to Mandurah in 1999 to see out his retirement.

To keep busy he was doing a few odd jobs around town when he heard about Kim's Toyboys. He stopped in to see them and started straight away making toys.

He was known to be a stickler for detail and could not stand to see toys not finished off properly. While he had his own shed he only made toys when he was at Kim's Toyboys premises.

Eric Rawlinson -   Joined in September 2001 and left in April 2005.

He spent most of his working life in Geraldton with Main Roads Department, Police Traffic Control and finally with the Council as a parking Inspector (35 years). In 2000 he retired and decided to move to Mandurah to be nearer to his wife Jackie's family.

He tried lawn bowls to keep him busy but decided it wasn't for him. His father-in-law (Peter Addison) talked him into joining with him at Kim's Toyboys. Eric had very little experience with woodworking but under the tuition of Peter he soon became very proficient. He not only attended at the Toyboys, but he had his own shed where he turned out most of the toys he made. He was like a human machine with number of toys he made.

Wood dust became a problem for him so he had to leave the Toyboys. He still kept in touch and even allowed them to store some timber in his shed. When asked for a comment on Men's Shed he said he thought they were a "necessary evil". Strange comment? He then explained "Men's Sheds are necessary to provide a venue where retirees can be kept busy doing something useful. The evil comes in if men are allowed to use machinery they are not competent with and accidents occur".

Barry Beament joined late in the year. He had just got back from an overseas trip and was looking for something to keep himself busy. He called into Lottery House and saw some wooden aeroplanes on display. When he enquired as to where they came from he was directed to Kim Butcher.

As he had his own shed and was into woodworking he was a welcome addition to the group. Barry easily fell into the production of toys and became a valuable member. As Toyboys did not meet very often he continued toy output in his own workshop. He enjoyed making some of the more detailed toys such as bulldozers and tip trucks.

He remembers well the various moves they had to make over the years. From Kim's home to the Senior Citizens building to Community First to John Tonkin College. He recalled all the packing up and cleaning up they had to do with each move. It was all part of being a Toyboy and never regretted any of it.

Apart from helping underprivileged families with toys, the camaraderie was what he enjoyed most. "Every day was a laugh" he said.

Barry was one of the longest "serving" members and left for family reasons in 2016.

The following men were part of the development of the Toyboys, but unfortunately could not be contacted for information on their background.

Barry Keseling – Joined April 2001 and left in June 2002.
Alec Osbourne – Joined April 2001 and left in October 2002.

YEAR 2002

CHAPTER 7

At this stage there were some very helpful ladies lending a hand with admin duties;

Phyllis Hardy from Peel Volunteer Centre took on the Treasurer' job.

Sue Taylor continued as minute taker.

Suzy Perkins from Department of Community Development assisted with admin aspects when needed. The framework was now in place to develop Toyboys into a growing operation that was to become well known in the Mandurah area. This included attracting some new players to boost the toy making output.

The group recognized that as they now operated as a working group there should be more controls established. The aspects that were to be developed and documented were:

>A tool register (the precursor to an asset register).
>Quality assurance training.
>An accident report book.
>Machinery operating and safety instructions.
>New toy designs.

They came to the realisation that to work properly they had to bring in the necessary checks and balances. Kim in particular was determined to see the group develop into a tightly run well respected operation.

The situation with Public Liability Insurance became a concern as the current premises at Ormsby Terrace did not offer security in terms of the public, including Day Care children being able to enter at any time. It was not practical for everyone to keep a constant visual check of the open entry. For this reason the thoughts were once again to keep a lookout for better premises.

It transpired that Job Futures Work for the Dole heard about their plight and suggested they look at the Community First workshop premises in Cumberland Street, Mandurah. Kim and Paul Ellis were the delegation that met with the Community First CEO to see how they could work together.

Again, it was not ideal as the centre was shared by other organisations, but at least there was a separate room where they could work and store their tools. Toys and donated wood would have to be stored elsewhere. They required strict adherence to safety rules, protective clothing and machinery maintenance. Being a community centre Community First had to ensure that any operation there was not seen to be a commercial business. As there was still some toys being made at Kim's place and at some Toyboys homes, the sale of any toys could be handled from there.

After some fancy negotiations (the best being no rent) an agreement was reached and they moved into it in September with part of the operation. I'm not sure, but I feel that David Templeman may have had a hand in that.

The esteem in which Kim's Toyboys were held was shown when they made some children's tables and chairs for the Women's Refuge Home. As you can appreciate men were forbidden to enter the premises for obvious reasons, but the Toyboys were allowed on to the premises to install the goods, not just drop them at the gate.

Helping hand for refuge

EQUIPMENT needed urgently by Mandurah women's refuge can be bought with a $500 donation from Mandurah branch of the Save the Children Fund.

The refuge also needs baby and children's clothes and toys as well as adult clothing.

Local group Toy Boys has also helped the refuge with a selection of handcrafted children's furniture and toys.

Anyone wanting to donate items to the refuge can contact Trish on 9535 4775.

Mandurah branch of Save the Children Fund has also donated a similar sum to two Aboriginal groups — Baalap Nikaaitidjine and Gjindi Benang.

Toy Boys David Brown, Paul Ellis, Bill Bowen and Kim Butcher, Mandurah branch SCF president Kim Morgan, Trish McGowan and Toys Boys Alec Osborne and Bob Loftus with the dolls furniture and cheque.

YEAR 2002

Helping Hands Support Group lodged $200 with A1 Salvage and Hardware for the group to purchase supporting material that they may need. This amount was topped up by Helping Hands as needed.

The donation of old bicycles was not massive but the group was still able to provide some underprivileged families with the reconditioned product. A few were sold at $20 each.

In May the Toyboys set up a booth at the Performing Arts Centre Family Fun Day. A good selection of the toys they make was on display to let the public know what they were capable of. A popular part of the display was children participating in the gluing of wheels on to small toys and then keeping them. It was such a hit that it became a regular part of participation at future Fun Days or Festivals. A raffle proved to be a good money earner last year so was to be held again.

    First prize: A scale airport
    Second prize: Table and chairs
    Third prize; Dolls pram

The scale airport

FROM TOY BOYS TO SHED MEN

During the year over 800 toys were made and donated to:

    Parenting for Young Mums.
    Women's Refuge Centre.
    Salvation Army for distribution.
    Helping Hands for distribution
    Performing Arts Fun Day

To cap off a wonderful year Kim's Toyboys were awarded the Kim Beazley Award for excellence in community work. A very proud Kim Butcher was at Council Chambers to accept it.

Kim receives the award from Kim Beazley

YEAR 2003

CHAPTER 8

The start of a new year saw the long arm of the law reaching out to Kim's Toyboys. Relax; it was only a retired policeman looking for a place that might help keep him active.

Graeme Gordon was Police Inspector at the Bunbury Police Station and decided that after 35 years in the Force it was time to retire. It was September 2001.

He and his wife Merlene were building a new home in Mandurah so it was the perfect time to make a move. He signed up for New Start which required him to either look for employment or do community work. He had just got out of a job so didn't want another one.

He started doing volunteer bus driving but then heard through the Peel Volunteer Centre that a group called Kim's Toyboys did woodworking and were looking for starters. This suited Graeme as he was already a keen woodworker. He had a talk with Kim and as they say "the rest is history".

Graeme started in February 2003 and not being one to stand back, became Vice Chairman in July of that year. A role he was to hold until 2019.

He became one of the most respected members of the group with his knowledge of regulations, business acumen and level headedness in decision making.

Colin Baker was the logistics manager for Arnetts before going into retirement. He is an avid gardener but wanted something else to help fill in his time. The Volunteer Centre had a list of places where community work could be carried out. He ran his finger down the list and when he came to Kim's Toyboys, he thought to himself "That will do me nicely".

He had a chat with Kim and became one of the Boys. His woodworking ability was a bit basic, but had a flare for working with his hands. With a bit of tuition he was soon turning out toys as good as anyone.

He is not sure how it happened but he became the "expert" on making dolls cots. There were basic ones, rocking ones and swinging ones. You name it he was your man.

Colin is also one of the early Toyboys who is still a member of the Men's Shed today.

Bevan Stephens joined the group in March. Not a lot is known about him except that he was originally a train driver.

When a new toy was developed he was remembered as often saying "You had better make an extra three for me". Guess who had three grandchildren?

He moved to Tasmania in 2006.

Ken Sawyer worked for a "Bunnings" type outlet in Manjimup before moving to Mandurah. His knowledge of hardware made him a perfect person to join the Toyboys, which he did in November.

He lived 25 kilometres outside of Mandurah and the travelling got too much for him after a while. He left in 2005.

Once again I had no luck contacting the following men to get their background.

Pat Robinson -   Joined March 2003 and left in September 2004.
Tom Callaghan – Joined April 2003 and left in October 2009.

CHAPTER 9

It is interesting that there are some things that never seem to change. One of those things is the continual need to replace dowel. Of all the support items that are needed in producing toys, dowel is the most constantly in demand. When looking at the toys that are made we see that a great number of them have wheels and axles. Hence, the need for dowel.

Through the years of the Toyboys and the Men's Shed this has always been the case. Although, one of the members was heard to remark "Are you sure someone isn't eating the stuff?".

Men of many talents!

YEAR 2003

The storage of toys was becoming a problem. The work areas barely allowed the Boys to make their toys, so toys were stored in Kim's home. Coodanup Family House was controlled by the Department of Child Protection, and they offered the use of a shed on the property. It did need a good clean out but was readily accepted. In the long term they would need something more practical, so it will stop Kim's house bursting at the seams.

Barry Beament to the rescue! He offered to have the area at the back of his shed available to be extended to provide storage for timber. This was readily accepted and a working bee was arranged to construct it. Pioneer Concrete generously donated the concrete.

Some of the toys at Kim's house

FROM TOY BOYS TO SHED MEN

In an effort to defray costs, particularly in relation to insurance cover, members were now charged $1.00 per week to attend. There were some questions as to what it actually covered, but in the main they were all okay with it.

The Annual General Meeting was held in July with the following being elected as office bearers;

>   Chairperson – Kim Butcher
>   Vice Chairperson – Graeme Gordon
>   Treasurer – Phylis Hardy
>   Secretary – David Brown
>   Minute Secretary – Sue Taylor

The storage of repaired bicycles was becoming a problem with few people wanting them. There was a fair flow of bicycles being donated but the demand going out was a problem. Plus, there was a probable need to purchase spare parts and that would be costly.

The Salvation Army helped out by taking a few for distribution to needy families. It was finally decided that the repairing of bicycles would be suspended.

Child Safe Australia was a big supporter of Kim's Toyboys. In appreciation of the happiness that they bring to children, they donated a great supply of timber. It was believed that without their support the Toyboys would not be able to produce the amount of toys they did.

The meetings introduced a new segment called "Show and Tell". A lot of the Toyboys had their own workshop and made some incredible items. The idea was to explain the workings of the item and discuss if it could be made by others to become part of stock. It turned out that almost all of the items were very detailed and took a long time to make so the segment petered out after 12 months.

In addition to making toys the Toyboys also took on special projects to help out community groups. The timber for the project would often be supplied, but if there was a need to provide material a small charge would often be made. Labour would be provided free. Such a project was for the Peel Youth Programme. They had a shed that needed shelving. They provided the timber and the Boys put it together.

Halls Head Primary School found that many of their students were showing an interest in chess. Teacher Steve Heighton had a bright idea and approached parents and the P&C to fund the building of a giant chess board on a concrete base. Having raised the funds they approached Kim's Toyboys to make it. The funds raised were $750 which they donated to the Toyboys. The Toyboys had never tackled anything like this before and were tickled pink with the outcome. The finished product was marvellous.

YEAR 2003

Overgrown chess table lures the children

by Narelle Butcher

THERE'S a new fad sweeping Halls Head Primary School. Chess has a class of year six students so enthralled the school campaigned to have a larger than life chess set built.

Teacher Steve Heighton said all students were interested in the game.

"The children expressed a huge interest in playing chess last term so we asked our Parents and Citizens if they wanted to assist with funds in creating a large chess board from paving slabs and purchasing matching chess pieces," Mr Heighton said.

The campaign to find the chess set was a collaborative effort between P and C president Mark Barrett and teachers Mr Heighton and Trish Petchell.

The search for the pieces led to local charity group Kim's Toy Boys – the brainchild of Kim Butcher.

Mr Butcher began the charity group more than two years ago and is dedicated to manufacturing toys for underprivileged children.

Last year, his group of 11 volunteers made 830 toys.

"Most of our products go to the Department of Community Development and they, in return, distribute them to their wards," Mr Butcher said.

"It makes a few children happy, particularly at Christmas."

Kim's Toy Boys produce wooden products such as prams, trains and cots. They also repair pushbikes.

Mr Butcher said all of his products were donated and the group relied on local businesses to donate materials such as timber.

He said it was the first chess set he had ever made.

Halls Head Primary School donated funds to Kim's Toy Boys as a token of their appreciation.

TIME TO PLAY: Students Adam Hobson, 11, and Kiara Halford, 10, encourage Kim's Toy Boys' Kim Butcher and teacher Steve Heighton to play chess.

The City of Mandurah ran a "Created Fun Day" in October which was a precursor to the Little Nippers Festival and then the Children's Festival that is conducted these days. The site was Hall Park on the western shore and Kim's Toyboys were invited to have a stall there. This was an opportune time to be able to promote the toys that were available for sale.

A selection of toys was made that would appeal to both boys and girls. Care was taken to ensure that the toys were of a basic design as these seem to appeal to children rather something that was intricate.

It was not only a big hit with the children, but parents and grandparents found an avenue where they could buy Xmas presents at a price that did not break the bank. In years to come this time of the year proved to be the busiest time for Kim's Toyboys, and then the Men's Shed, in selling toys. The word was starting to spread about the Toyboys.

Wide eyed boys check out the toys

YEAR 2003

It was estimated that approximately 1,800 toys were produced during the year. Toys donated throughout the year were given to:

- Malibu School
- Zonta House
- Bingee Busters Aboriginal Group
- Women's Refuge
- Over 50's Dance Group
- Make A Wish
- Department of Community Development

The Toyboys group is starting to grow

YEAR 2004

CHAPTER 10

John Boulton. Apart from a couple of years running a lunch bar, John was a carpenter until he retired. After a few years living in Lake Clifton he and Irene decided to see out their days in Mandurah.

Although he was primarily a "chippy" he was also a dab hand at making wooden items, whether it be furniture, decorations, kids toys etc.

When he went to register at Centrelink, they suggested that he do some sort of community work. They saw he was a carpenter and recommended he have a talk with Kim's Toyboys. He had a talk with Kim and found it was an opportune time as they were looking to increase their numbers.

He soon became an integral part of the Toyboys as his nature was that he would hop in and get involved in all parts of their day to day workings. His involvement became such, that when Kim took a step back from the Toyboys in 2009, he handed the Chairmanship to John.

He led the group through some interesting times and put his heart and soul into making sure operations ran smoothly. His forte was in making some of the larger special projects. He soon became known as the person to contact about Shed operations.

Frank O'Malley. Joined February 2004 and left in May 2007. I tried hard but could not find Frank to get some background info on him.

CHAPTER 11

Phyllis Hardy advised the group that she had to resign from the Treasurer position as she was off sailing. Mark Perkins agreed to take on the job. It was hoped that a Toyboy would take on the job at a later time, so it was wait and see.

The stockpile of toys was growing all the time. The Toyboys were relentless, just wind them up, let them go and they kept churning out toys.

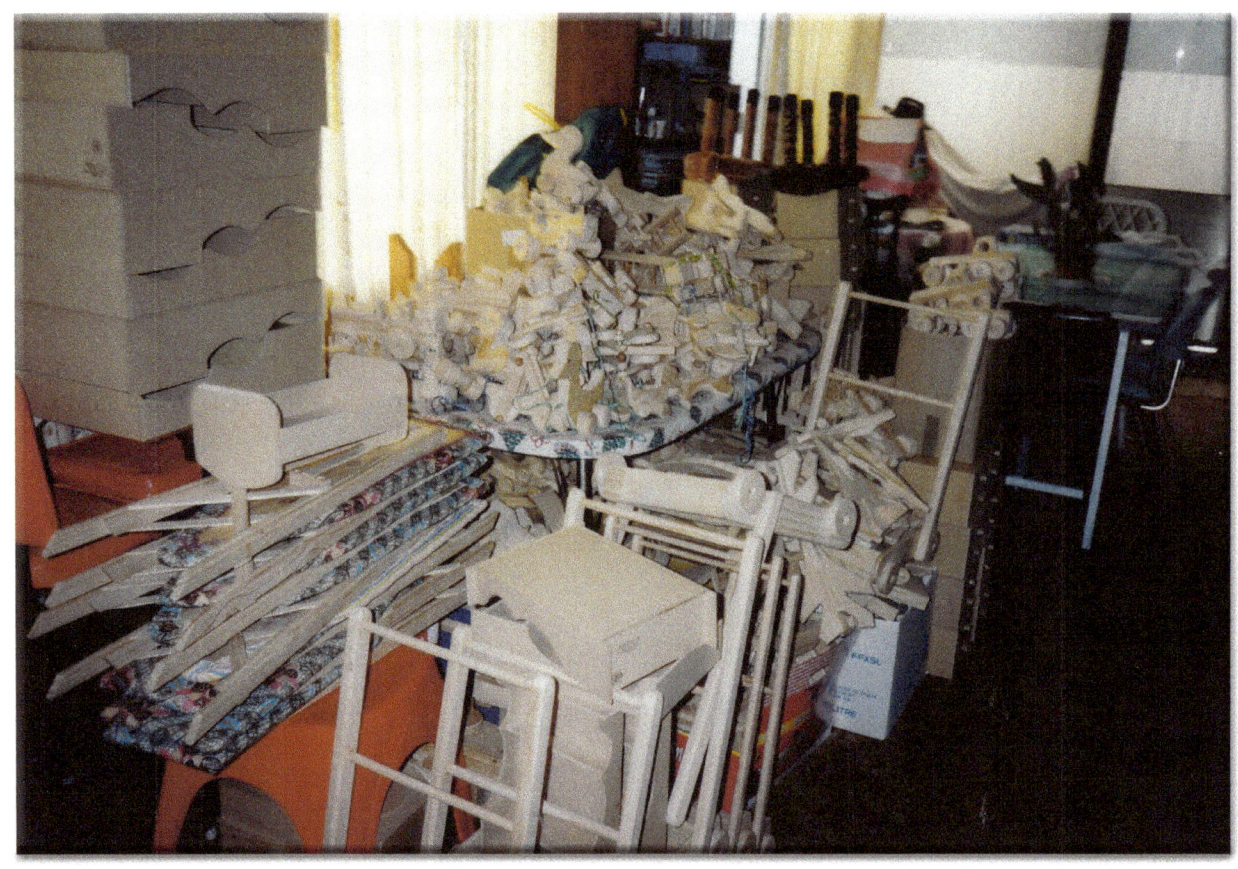

The stockpile of toys keeps growing

YEAR 2004

The shed at Coodanup House was now a big help with the storage of toys, but they still kept a wary eye pealed for a permanent answer.

Mirvac Fini conducted Community Development Fund Awards and this year Kim's Toyboys was one of the recipients. It was in the form of a cash payment which solved their problem of paying for the ever increasing premium for insurance cover. There was a bit left over so a new drill set was purchased.

The AGM was a quiet affair as for some unknown reason most of the Toyboys could not attend. The elected office bearers were a continuation with Mark Perkins being named as Treasurer.

The Wood Turners Association held a workshop at the Mandurah High School and the Toyboys were invited to display some of their handiwork. This was a great opportunity to promote the group and the toys that were made. The raffle of a small rocking horse raised a few dollars.

A few cracks were starting to appear in the arrangements with Community First. They wanted the Toyboys to change their name to Peel Activity Group. This took away the identity of the Toyboys and was not acceptable. There were to be strict rules on the wearing of steel boots, earmuffs and safety glasses. In fairness to them, they were going to supply those items. Safety gear was to be worn when using machinery.

A cupboard was to be provided for Toyboys to store some materials and tools. Wood could not be stored and toys could not be sold from the premises. They wanted to be consulted with the distribution of toys from the premises.

The controlling net seemed to be tightening around them. But, no way was Kim going to hand over the controls. Happy to be there with no rent and some funding, but always had in the back of his mind that some other suitable premises could pop up.

No point in waiting too long though. It was suggested that the large shed at the Silver Chain might be able to accommodate their operation. Enquiries were made with them but it did not pan out. The Lions Club premises were also a consideration, but alas no go again.

The Little Nipper's Festival was well attended and the Toyboys marquee was very popular. They decided that when they attended the next Festival they would need a bigger marquee and more trestles. A bigger site would mean that more free toys could be given away to kids.

Toyboy toys pop up in the most unexpected places. The Performing Arts Centre was presenting the pantomime Pinocchio and guess whose toys were used as stage props? Yep, you guessed it.

You may recall I wrote earlier about the "Show and Tell" segment? Well, Brent Taylor showed a 4 wheel drive vehicle and Kim a buggy. Alas, they were to be the last as this segment was discontinued.

During the year toys were donated to:

- Pat Thomas memorial House
- Zonta Club
- Make-A-Wish
- Nullagine and Halls Creek community centres (DCD)
- Save Our Seniors
- Child Care Centre Boddington
- Milligan Foundation
- Peel Community Legal Service
- Silver Chain

YEAR 2005

CHAPTER 12

Jack Williams worked for the PMG line section fixing cables and overhead wires until he retired. Like most retirees he took himself off to Centrelink who told him that to get Newstart funding he needs to do some community work.

His good friend Lew Hanna had heard about Kim's Toyboys and suggested he have a talk to them. So, off he went and had a talk to Kim, liked what they were about and started the next week.

While Jack had some basic skills in working with wood he preferred to stick with the smaller type of toys. Band saws and planners were OK with him but for some reason he didn't like to use the drop saw and lathe.

Jack loved the idea that we made hundreds of small toys to give to children at Festivals. He took on the role of coordinating the production of these toys and cracked the whip when it was necessary. Because of him we never ran short of toys that brought a smile to the faces of hundreds of kids.

One of the small toys that was popular with the kids was a helicopter. Jack started making them himself to top up the numbers but liked them so much he just kept on making them. He soon became known to the boys as the "helicopter man".

He had such an easy going nature that you couldn't help but like him. He had the knack of saying things that the boys weren't sure whether he was joking or not. Would just walk away and leave them wondering.

It was a dark day in September 2019 when the Shed was told the news that Jack had had a massive stroke and did not survive. One of life's gentlemen gone.

CHAPTER 13

As the numbers were gradually growing it was decided to hold future Kim's Toyboys meetings at The Department of Community Development offices, as theirs was more roomy and comfortable.

There is no doubt that there were a lot of benefits by working at Community First. There was no rent payable, safety gear was provided, work boots supplied and even some T-shirts and polo shirts. On the negative side though, they were still keen to have the name of Kim's Toyboys changed to represent what Community First was about. It didn't happen.

A Community First supervisor had to be present. Some days Toyboys were prevented from attending as no supervisor was available. This caused a few niggles as Toyboys were not advised in advance. Any tools funded by Community First became their property. There was a grey area with insurance. It was not clear what the Community First covered compared to the Toyboys cover.

Agreed, it was not an ideal arrangement, but as there was nothing else in the offering the Toyboys made the best of it.

Wood was again becoming a problem. No wood, no toys. The feelers were put out to suss out what they might be able to get. Brent Taylor kept up scrounging at building sites but they needed lots more wood. Thankfully All Pine Timber and Hardware came to the party and donated some timber which helped in the short term.

In amongst all this there was something that was always constant, barbecue get-togethers at Kim and Bettys place. It was important to Kim to keep the morale of the boys at a high level. More often than not they supplied the meat and drinks with the boys (or their wives more likely) the salads. They put some on during the year and always for the Xmas break up.

In addition to the Women's Refuge Centre Kim's Toyboys were happy to support the

FROM TOY BOYS TO SHED MEN

Pat Thomas House which also ran a domestic violence service. Their child's support room needed some toys so the Toyboys couldn't wait to step forward and help out. It was being part of this community spirit that made the Toyboys proud.

Toy makers help out

by Narelle Butcher

PAT Thomas House's new child support room was given a boost last week by local toy makers, Kim's Toyboys.

The volunteer group donated dozens of wooden toys to the domestic violence service to bring joy to children.

Pat Thomas House coordinator Trish McGowan said the donation was a case of local organisations helping each other.

The child's support room is an additional service provided by Pat Thomas House which has been operating since January.

Ms McGowan said it provided a safe haven for children affected by domestic violence.

"With additional funding provided by the Department of Community Development, we have been able to provide the new service," she said.

"Now all the children in the residence service can use this room.

"Primarily it aims to provide a room for children where they can freely express themselves and forget about the other things going on in their lives."

TOYS GALORE: Kim's Toyboys coordinator Kim Butcher donated wooden toys to Pat Thomas House coordinator Trish McGowan and child support worker, Jodi (front).

Kim's Toyboys coordinator Kim Butcher said the volunteers worked tirelessly throughout the year to help bring joy to children.

The group makes wooden toys for underprivileged children that are distributed by the Department of Community Development.

Items donated to Pat Thomas House include trucks and trains, dolls cots, rocking horses and chairs.

YEAR 2005

The Toyboys were invited to have a stall at the Greenfields Family Centre Kids Fun Day which they accepted. These types of events were proving to be most beneficial as they not only promoted the name Kim's Toyboys but provided an avenue to sell some toys and boost the coffers.

The central part of our stall however, was the provision of small toys onto which the children were shown how to insert axles and glue the wheels on. Once done the child could take the toys at no cost.

A relatively small thing but you should have seen the smiles on the kids' faces. On the day, about 300 toys were given away, but it could have been a lot more if they knew how popular this would be with the children.

Kids getting a toy with glued wheels

Kim believed that publicity plays a big part in the progress of any operation. He was very successful in getting a number of articles in the local newspapers, but encouraged the Toyboys to keep an eye out for any avenues that they could take advantage of.

FROM TOY BOYS TO SHED MEN

Toys were donated during the year to;

- Milligan Foundation
- Silver Chain
- Zonta Club
- Department of Community Development Rockingham
- Women's Refuge House
- Pat Thomas House
- Salvation Army
- Make-A-Wish

ND STRUCTURE REPRESENTATIONS

YEAR 2006

CHAPTER 14

Len Burton was a farmer in Harvey for many years and finally retired in Mandurah.

He was well known at the Perth Royal Show as the man who could turn his hand to many things and was basically "Mr. Fixit".

Len's preferred skill was carpentry and when he heard about Kim's Toyboys he called in and had a talk to Kim. He liked the idea of making kid's toys so was accepted into the Toyboys in May.

He was a real asset to the group because his many skills helped if there was a breakdown with machinery or something needed fixing.

He was with the Toyboys until 2012.

Despite actively seeking new members, Len was the only new Toyboy this year.

Wood was once again in short supply. Urgent messages were sent out to local builders seeking donations of wood. Some of the Toyboys were travelling to country areas to collect dressed timber that became available. Never a dull moment at the Shed!

More meetings with Community First! Safety needs and supervision were back on the agenda. It was felt that Community First was trying to take more control of the Toyboys operation. That was never going to happen.

A Memorandum of Understanding was drawn up and given to Kim for consideration. As there were a number of items that were not acceptable it looked like being a while before agreement would be reached.

In general, the activities of the Toyboys just concentrated on building up the stock of toys that were to satisfy the usual heavy demand before Xmas. Special projects were at a minimum which left all the gang to make toys.

YEAR 2006

There was one special project this year however, that was a real eye opener.

At a meeting, Colin Baker brought up the fact that Prince Frederick of Denmark and Princess Mary had a new son Prince Christian. "So what?" was the response.

Being the patriotic type Colin replied "Princess Mary is an Australian, so I think we should make a gift for Prince Christian. It should be typically Australian, say a rocking kangaroo made out of jarrah". The meeting agreed, and gave Colin the job of making the "Rocky Roo".

Before work commenced letters were exchanged between the Toyboys and the Danish Embassy to ensure they would be happy to accept it. The answer came back that they would be delighted to receive it. The finished product was a credit to Colin and worthy of a Prince.

Air freight was going to cost $1,200 with Qantas but negotiated down to $600. Still a bit pricey, so Kim Beazley, David Templeman and the City of Mandurah shared that cost between them.

Kangaroo for Prince

A BABY prince on the other side of the world will soon have an Australian toy.

Mandurah group Kim's Toy-Boys have made a jarrah rocking kangaroo as a gift to Prince Christian of Denmark from the Mandurah community after the Palace accepted their offer of a gift.

Mandurah MLA David Templeman and Brand MHR Kim Beazley helped pay for the safe passage of the "rocky roo" to Denmark.

Kim's ToyBoys makes handmade wooden toys and donates them to charities and disadvantaged children.

To make a donation or materials, call Kim Butcher on 9535 5802.

Mandurah MLA David Templeman and Brand MHR Kim Beazley and Kim's Toyboys members admire the wooden rocking kangaroo.

The Rocky Roo was sent to Denmark as coming from the Mandurah community. The Danish Embassy sent a letter confirming that it had been received with pleasure, but declined the request of a photo of the little Prince and the Rocky Roo,

Toys were donated during the year to:

    Fairbridge Farm
    Pemberton School
    Rockingham Lakes School
    Boddington Toy Library
    Dwellingup Playgroup
    Peel Health Campus
    Dudley Park Primary School

YEAR 2007

CHAPTER 15

Barry Carter too was a farmer and when he retired to Mandurah was accepted into Kim's Toyboys not long after Len Burton.

He was a man of generous proportions and the other Toyboys could not believe it when they learned he was an accomplished sportsman. I could not confirm where, but I believe he was Club Champion for six years running at a Golf Club in the South West.

Barry was with the Boys until October 2009.

Neville Barker was the next to join the group.

Neville was a retired police office and was an avid woodworker in his leisure time. He worked as a police diver and resulting lung problems forced him into retirement.

When he heard about the Toyboys he felt it was the most natural place for him to join. His crowning glory was the making of a clock entirely out of wood. He too left the group in October 2009.

CHAPTER 16

The Toyboys felt that holding a meeting every month ate into their toy making time too much as they only met twice a week. It was agreed that meetings would now be held every two months, unless there was a special need to discuss a particular issue.

Wood, wood, wood! A constant thorn in their side but without it their operation was doomed. Forever needing to seek supplies of both dressed and undressed timber (to non-woodworking readers that means not planed smooth – not nude).

When supplies are obtained, where to store it? And, there was the ever dwindling supply of dowel.

Undaunted the Toyboys carried on and never lost their enthusiasm. There always seemed to be something to get them through. A toy sale or two, a small grant from a community centre or just receiving a donation. They never lost heart, as they believed that Kim's Toyboys played an important part in filling a service that the community needed.

Issues between Community First and Kim's Toyboys seemed to be resolved and a new Memorandum of Understanding was signed.

The early start to the year saw the Art in the Sand Festival. It had primarily a summer theme for all the displays but invites were sent to various community groups to have a tent and promote their operation.

The Toyboys were invited and were happy to accept. Here was an opportunity to sell a few toys and wooden train "donation" boxes were a drawcard. This combination brought in a welcome amount of funds.

The Greenfields Community Centre was again holding their Festival and the Toyboys agreed to participate once more. This was one of those opportunities to sell a few toys for funds to replace timber. More importantly, they were able to provide kids with the small toys they were able to glue wheels on.

A busy time at the Toyboys stand

Susie Taylor advised the group that she was leaving and had to give up the minute taking. Suzie and Mark Perkins advised that they were leaving DCD too. What a dilemma, no Secretary and no Treasurer.

John Boulton, always ready to help, put up his hand and said "I know someone who will do it, my wife Irene." What a guy! He then went home and told Irene what she had been dobbed in for.

Knowing what John was like it did not faze her and took it in her stride. She had previous office administration experience and did the books for her last job at Retravision. She didn't tell John, but really welcomed taking on the job as Secretary/Treasurer as she was no longer working. This now gave her an interest.

They were not hard jobs to take over as the records and books were well kept and she just had to "follow the bouncing ball" as the saying goes. Being more involved it was now an opportunity the meet more of the wives or partners and work with them on activities behind the scenes.

The City of Mandurah had been very good to the Toyboys in providing some funding from time to time. When the City approached Kim to cut out some boomerangs for

Little Nippers to paint at the Festival he was happy to do it. He asked "How may do you want made?" and the answer was "1,000". Kim picked himself up off the floor, shook his head and said "Why not".

This was the start of what was to become a close relationship with the Events Team at the City of Mandurah. Many of the events they held required some sort of wooden "items". Jobs were offered to the Toyboys and in most cases they were able to help. Sometimes the Events Team had a budget for items and Kim would quote them a price. The quotes were nowhere near what a commercial price would be. It was a win-win situation.. The Toyboys were becoming rather adept at satisfying unusual requests.

The Mandurah Food Bank coordinated a Christmas Appeal for underprivileged families every year and Kim's Toyboys were a major contributor with toys. It was not only a great feeling for the Toyboys in doing something worthwhile, but it certainly helped to reduce the growing stack of toys.

Loading up over 400 toys

FROM TOY BOYS TO SHED MEN

The Mandurah Croquet and Recreation Club approached Kim with a request for something a little different. They were trying to start a junior section in their club, but the croquet clubs they had were too big. "Could the Toyboys make some smaller ones" they asked.

Without missing a beat, Kim replied "Yep, we can do that". Before you know it, the boys had knocked out ten small croquet mallets for the Club

During the year toys were donated to;

    Zonta Club
    Smith Family Group
    Dawesville Catholic Primary School
    Baptist Church
    Pat Thomas House

YEAR 2008

CHAPTER 17

This was a relatively quiet year for the Toyboys as it was generally "business as usual".

There were no new members despite feelers being put out to a few community groups where retirees might be.

There was one bright start to the year. On Australia Day the City of Mandurah awarded Achievement Certificates to various community groups for the excellent work done to support underprivileged families and the community in general. This year one was awarded to Kim's Toyboys.

YEAR 2008

Kim's health was getting a few cracks in it as the dust in the workshop was affecting his lungs. He hinted that it might be time to hand over the reins.

The Little Nippers festival was gaining popularity and the Toyboys were happy to be part of it. This was shaping up to be the single best fund raiser we were having each year. Every effort was made to keep the kids happy with give-away toys while the parents and grandparents were kept busy checking out the toys for sale.

A steady stream of "customers"

Toys donated this year went to;

    Peaceful Children's Home Kenya
    Baptist Church
    Mandurah Garden Club
    Falcon Primary School
    Pemberton District School
    Salvation Army
    Rotary Club of Mandurah Districts
    Zonta Club

Genesis Counselling and Training supported disadvantaged overseas communities and approached Kim's Toyboys to ask if they could supply some small toys. The children of Peaceful Children's Home in Kenya were to be the recipients. They would then paint them to their own design. The report back from Genesis was that the children were thrilled to receive them and could not believe their luck in getting such "treasures".

Just look at those smiles?

YEAR 2009

CHAPTER 18

Aik Wee Goh is a pastor who travelled regularly to Malaysia to help rehabilitate drug addicts and "fallen" women. To be accepted back into society though, they had to be able to show they had a skill that could be of benefit to the community. (Who's that you ask? We know him as **Rudy Goh**).

He started by teaching them fishing skills but felt this was not enough. If they had to have a skill that allowed them to make a product, that product could be sold at one of the local markets.

Something made out of wood seemed to be a good choice as timber was readily available. He heard about a group in Mandurah that made some terrific toys, so decided to approach them. Rudy called in on spec and talked with John Boulton and Jack Williams. He must have touched their hearts, because although he told them he had no woodworking experience, they welcomed him into the group

He was a quick learner and was soon able to produce commendable toys. His new found skill was taken to Malaysia and put to good use. Wheels for some toys were not as good as he liked so he learnt how to use a lathe to turn out wheels. He has become so proficient on the lathe that he is now considered to be one of two "gurus" at the Men's Shed who produce wood turning.

Although he lives in Kenwick, he still travelled each week to the Shed. He summed up the Men's Shed as "A great bunch of people who are willing to teach a greener than green learner".

Rudy left the shed in 2020 due to his parish commitments.

CHAPTER 19

The hint that was given out last year had now come to be fact. Kim decided that due to his health issues it was time to pass on the position of Chairman.

Kim steps down from toy duty

KIM Butcher has handed over the presidency of toy making group Kim's Toy Boys to John Bolton.

Mr Bolton will ensure the group continues to make wooden toys for disadvantaged children and charitable organisations.

Mr Butcher, now 75, started the group with other retirees after he retired from the workforce.

The group started making toys in Mr Butcher's home workshop in 1999 before relocating to an Ormsby Terrace facility two years later.

Members now meet twice a week at the Community First building to make toys including trucks, doll houses and rocking horses.

Mr Bolton said the non-profit group made between 2000-3000 toys annually.

Mr Butcher, and his wife Betty, were presented a plaque from the Toy Boys to commemorate his years of dedication to the group.

Community groups or schools can request toys by contacting Mr Bolton on 0410 105 498.

The big question was, who to hand it to? There were several Toyboys who had been with Kim for some time so the decision was not made lightly.

The final decision was John Boulton. John had shown that he was dedicated to the job of providing toys and was unrivalled at the Toyboys in carpentry and woodworking. It wasn't just wood he was experienced in as he had a very good knowledge of machinery and tools.

This wasn't to be the last of Kim though. "My resignation from the Chair doesn't mean you won't see me again. I'll be in to give you hell from time to time" he said.

Kim hands over the reins

To show their appreciation Graeme Gordon made a plaque from a jarrah burl that they presented to Kim.

YEAR 2009

The plaque reads:

Presented to
Kim Butcher
Founder of Kim's Toy Boys Inc.
In appreciation of your loyal service to the group
2009

The Annual General Meeting was held and the new office bearers were;

　　Chairman – John Boulton
　　Vice Chairman – Graeme Gordon
　　Treasurer/Secretary – Irene Boulton

There was now a dedicated team with John and Irene, together with Graeme as a great sounding board.

The Moora Arts and Crafts Group invited the Toyboys to attend their Expo in July. They wanted their members to be shown how the toys were made with the hope that they could reproduce them.

A check with the Boys found that there were four couples who wanted to attend. Kim booked four sites and off they went in a convoy of caravans to invade the town of Moora. The weekend proved to be successful on several fronts.

First, they were able to show the crafts group some new ideas on toy making. Toys were taken in kit form to show how they were put together. Second, they were able to sell a few of their toys, which always helps. Third, they had a most enjoyable time on a social level. It was really good for them to break from routine.

There was some good news on the funding side with a grant of $4,000 being approved under the Government Volunteer Grants 2009. This enabled the Toyboys to install some extra machinery that will make their jobs much easier. It was also funding to tackle the dust problem that had always been a concern to members.

On receiving the letter of approval the Toyboys could not contain themselves, hopping around with the thought of going to Bunnings like the proverbial kids in a candy store.

The Toyboys participated again this year with the Little Nippers Festival conducted by the City of Mandurah. They were able to display a good variety of toys and sold over thirty of them on the day. The pleasing aspect was that people donated over $500 to the Toyboys during the day. This indicated the people are recognising the great work that Kim and the boys do for the community.

Donations this year were to:

    3 Day Care Centres
    Mandurah Primary School Kindergarten
    Friends of Peel Hospital
    Hilton-Hamilton Community
    Shelley Primary School
    Retired Police Officers Association

Christmas is a special time for the Toyboys as this is when a big amount of their toys go out to kids.

YEAR 2009

In a good Claus

THEY don't want to know who has been good and who has been bad in this Santa's workshop in Mandurah; all they really want to know is that the toys they make put smiles on to children's faces.

The workers in this Santa's workshop, or Kim's Toyboys as they are more commonly known, are a group of retired gentlemen who were brought together by Santa – or Kim Butcher as he is more commonly known, seven years ago.

When Kim first got the men together, their aim was to make wooden toys for underprivileged children, but in recent years, it has gone beyond that.

"We produce more than 2000 wooden toys per year," Kim said.

"We make just about everything – trucks, tractors, cars, cots, chairs, tables and rocking horses.

"Our toys have been sent everywhere from Halls Creek to England – we even sent a Rocky Roo to Prince Christian in Denmark when he was born."

For the full story on the Toyboys, look out for the first edition of our *Older and Wiser* magazine, due out on December 13.

Your child could have a toy fit for a king, with Kim's Toyboys donating a Rocky Roo to go to a lucky *Lifestyle Mandurah* reader.

Kim Butcher surrounded by his 'elves'. Below: Kim Butcher and Rocky Roo.

d235679

All you have to do is tell us in 25 words or less why someone you know deserves to have Rocky Roo under their Christmas tree. Send entries to Rocky Roo, *Lifestyle Mandurah*, PO Box 33, Mandurah, or hand deliver to *Mandurah Coastal Times*, Unit 2, 96 Pinjarra Rd, by Thursday, December 20.

YEAR 2010

CHAPTER 20

Alas, another quiet year for attracting new members. No takers.

The quality of toys being made once again raised its head. It was essential that the finished products be of a good quality if the Toyboys were to maintain their reputation with the general public. John and Graeme kept an eye on this aspect.

There were a growing number of people offering unwanted used timber to the Toyboys. This was welcomed as they could dress it down for use, but as more came in storage was becoming a problem. John Moore Builders were providing offcuts which added to the problem.

The Lions Club of Mandurah wanted to establish a memorial to one of their most respected club members. They approached Kim and asked if the Toyboys could make a cabinet to hold memorabilia. As Kim was getting used to unusual requests now, he once more said yes and they soon had it done.

The situation at Community First was not improving and the Boys were just plodding along to keep the wheels turning. Their heart was not in it to keep operating from that venue. The atmosphere had not improved and the feeling was that the sooner they could find alternative premises the better.

It wasn't through lack of trying though, as John and Graeme kept following up on any leads that cropped up. They were determined to find something and not let the Boys down.

It was Little Nippers Festival time again and the boys had been busy churning out toys. They were feeling good about the variety and amount of stock that had been produced.

Unfortunately, there was not a big attendance at the Festival. Although there was a threat of bad weather, it did not eventuate and this probably kept the people at home. Although not our best take, we still had reasonable sales on the day. Oh well, you can't win 'em all.

All stocked up and ready to go

Toys donated this year went to an ever growing number of recipients;

    Peel Health Paediatric Wing
    Rock Bay
    Bedington Lodge
    Make-A-Wish
    Reheboth Christian College
    Moora Community Health
    Mandurah Garden Club
    Rafiki Surgical Missions
    Nannup Child Care
    Relay for Life (Cancer)

YEAR 2011

CHAPTER 21

Lew Hanna worked for Telecom (NOT Telstra he will tell you) for many years until he was made redundant. He and Zingra decided to have a break and spent a few weeks travelling around before returning to home base. NEC had taken over ALCOA and invited Lew to join them, which he did until he retired.

His good friend Jack Williams had been involved for a few years with Kim's Toyboys and suggested Lew join them. It sounded like a good idea except……his woodworking skills weren't all that flash. He had made a few Mallee root tables but that was about it. Undaunted, he got into the business of making toys.

He had the unenviable reputation of having broken the most band saw blades. Whenever the sound of a saw blade breaking was heard the cry went up "Lew's here". He also became the self-appointed "tidy police". Lew was quick to point out if tools were left lying about or machinery not cleared of sawdust. Unfortunately this happened all too often.

Lew became a committee member and later took on the responsibility of coordinating the work of the two handicapped boys who come in once a week.

Bill Vardy worked in the industrial safety and emergency response areas of companies like BHP and Woodside until his retirement. After moving to Mandurah he thought a Men's Shed might be the go for him because, as he put it, he liked to "play with wood in his own shed".

His go-getter daughter-in-law soon had it sussed out and got him details for Kim's Toyboys. He spoke with John Boulton who said they had a new system for new members and would have to appear before a meeting of all existing members.

He did this and must have passed their "scrutiny" as he was accepted in to the fold.

Bill pointed out that this system was only ever used on him and never again! He is not sure what that means.

Bill is a "bit of an artist" as he put it, and when he saw one of the Toyboys making a hash of painting a toy he offered to take over. That was the start of him being given the job of any intricate painting required. He didn't mind though as he could do that in his spare time at home.

Although he made some standard toys his preference is making the larger type or completing special projects.

CHAPTER 22

As Kim's Toyboys was growing in numbers it was becoming increasingly harder to hold meetings with all members on a regular two monthly basis. It was decided therefore that the Chairman and Vice Chairman would deal with every day matters as they arose. A meeting would only be called when a special item had to be discussed with all members.

I'm not complaining mind you, but with fewer meetings it made it harder to research operations of the Toyboys. I now had to rely more on the recollections of the members and at our collective ages that can be a little challenging. Undaunted, the intrepid writer pushes on!

One such meeting of members was in regard to the introduction of club shirts. It was greeted favourably with just the matter of price and colour to discuss. Quotes were obtained and details put to the Boys.

Price was acceptable but colour was a point of contention. There was a split vote between maroon and blue. After quite some discussion maroon was agreed upon.

YEAR 2011

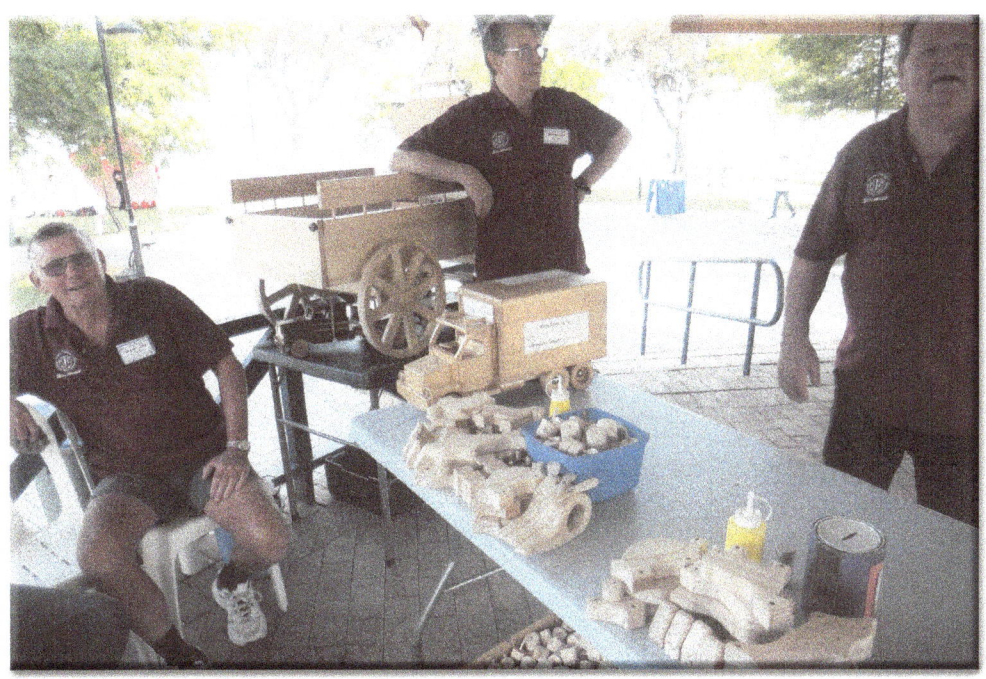

Colin, Paul and John show off the new shirts

Time was running out! The agreement with Community First was coming to an end and it was not going to be renewed. All efforts to find new premises did not turn up anything that was suitable. As a last resort they decided to try and get a "please help" newspaper article published.

Boys seek home

LOCAL Mandurah community group Kim's Toyboys is still seeking appropriate accommodation so they can continue their community work.

The group, which has been operating in Mandurah for more than 10 years, involves a group of men who every year make more than 3000 wooden toys for children including children from underprivileged families.

The group's patron and MLA David Templeman said Kim's Toyboys members had made a magnificent contribution to the community for many years.

"What we need is a large shed on a semi-rural site for about two days a week and the capacity to store our equipment and supplies," group president John Bolton said. Mr Templeman said they were appealing to anyone who had a suitable shed or even an unused industrial site for the community organisation to contact the office on 9581 3944 or Mr Bolton on 9535 1370.

Appeal for help: Kim's Toyboys members have sought help from David Templeman to secure a new home.

It was hoped that the combination of the City of Mandurah, David Templeman and the newspaper article will turn up something before they are put out into the street.

There was a group called the Doghouse Club which shared the Community First premises and made wooden items for their own use. They too were concerned that their time at those premises was limited. Accordingly, they aligned themselves with Kim's Toyboys and had joint meetings to monitor the situation.

As the sale of toys was beginning to wane it was suggested that perhaps the price of them was too high. All agreed and a review of the pricing was carried out.

To the uninitiated this would seem quite amazing, when you consider that the price of their toys was already some 50 to 70 percent below what a commercial price would be. Still, the show must go on.

Regardless of these issues, the production of toys had to be maintained. The Little Nippers Fun Day had been renamed to the Children's Festival and the Toyboys had to make sure this major fund raising day for them was ready to go.

Toys donated went to;

> Salvation Army
> Rafiki Group
> Esther Foundation
> Make-A-Wish
> Zonta Club

YEAR 2012

CHAPTER 23

With seeking, finding, moving and settling in with new premises not a lot of time was given to new membership so there was just one new starter.

Kevin Manning was a carpenter/cabinet maker who retired to Mandurah. He was an avid woodworker and built up his own shed where he made some beautiful model cars, trucks etc. He felt he would like to join an organisation where he could combine his woodworking with some companionship.

He heard about the Mandurah Men's Shed so popped in for a chat. He liked what he saw and joined, as it was like a home away from home.

Kevin slipped easily into becoming part of the toy production team. Almost by default, he became the "go to" man for a few items. They were a kiddie workbench, a learning tower (he called them a step-up) and kiddie chairs. He didn't only make these, as he produced other toys as the need arose. It was just that he made them so well that the others were happy to let him do it.

"The Shed is such a part of my life now I don't know what I would do if I couldn't come here" said Kevin.

CHAPTER 24

The City of Mandurah approached the Toyboys to make a picket fence to segregate an area in front of the stage for the Australia Day celebrations. Being used to odd requests from the Shire, they didn't bat an eyelid, just got into it and "hey presto" all done. They did politely decline a suggestion by the City that the Toyboys do the same picket fence either side of Mandurah Terrace all the way from the bridge to the roundabout.

The Toyboys now had to make all-out efforts to find new premises. Several leads were followed up, some promising, but none were what was needed. David Templeman became aware that the auto shop section of Mandurah High School (later to be John Tonkin College) was not being used and made enquiries with the school Principal Catherine Shepherd as to its suitability for the Toyboys.

Two big rooms to work from

FROM TOY BOYS TO SHED MEN

David took John Boulton and Graeme Gordon to have a look and asked them if they thought it would fit the bill. To say that John and Graeme were excited would be an understatement. They could not believe the amount of space that it provided. Not only could all Toyboys work there together on the same day but covered areas could be used for the storage of timber.

"I think I've died and gone to heaven" said John. Together with a delegation from Kim's Toyboys David met with the school Principal and arrived at a suitable working arrangement. The best being free rent and utilities.

The arrangements were that they could have access to the premises on four half days Tuesday to Friday. Initially this was set at Tuesday and Thursday mornings. For security reasons, everybody had to sign a daily attendance sheet which was then delivered to the school Administration.

The rooms however were in a bit of a mess. There were oil and auto parts all over the place, so there was nothing the Boys could do but to roll up their sleeves and clean up. It took them all week to do that with lots of elbow grease and many trips to the tip.

The school did not want any of the auto parts so the Toyboys even made a bit of money from scrap metal dealers.

Toy boys find a home

MANDURAH'S Toy Boys have found a home for the next 12 months at John Tonkin College in Gibla Street after an exhaustive search.

The Toy Boys are a group of men who, for more than a decade, have been making wooden toys for children and disadvantaged families.

The Toy Boys' current premises had come to an end and if a new home could not be found they were in danger of folding.

Toy Boys' patron Mandurah MLA David Templeman negotiated with the John Tonkin College principal Catherine Shepherd to have the group operate from the campus.

"This group of men has produced thousands of toys for children, many of them from needy families, for over a decade and I couldn't let them fold," Mr Templeman said. Ms Shepherd said the school more than happy to accommodate them for the next 12 months.

"It is hoped the group may be able to work in partnership with students from the school on some projects this year," Mr Templeman said.

The Toy Boys will work from the College's woodworking workshop and will now be able to continue to produce quality wooden toys for the local community.

President John Bolton said he appreciated the support the group had received from Mr Templeman, Ms Shepherd and Technology and Enterprise teacher Gavin Farbey.

Good news: David Templeman, Technology and Enterprise teacher Gavin Farbey and members of Kim's Toy Boys check out their new workshop. 16/2/2012

Once the place was cleaned there came the task of moving all their gear in. A lot of the Toyboys had dual cab vehicles so this helped. Convoys moved back and forth for a couple of days before it was done. The school had left some tools and supply items there so these were put into cupboards until the school claimed them (they were all still there eight years later).

The Doghouse Club threw themselves at the mercy of the Toyboys as they too had to move from Community First. They had nine members and a fair collection of tools and machinery. It was agreed that they could use our premises on a Friday afternoon as an autonomous group.

In February the Toyboys moved into their new home and they settled in to what they hoped would be a long, long stay. The arrangements worked well except – toilets! The Toyboys were only able to use the toilets used by the school staff. This meant a trek down to Administration, get the key, complete the "visit", return the key and trek back. This was a bit wearing on elderly legs so an alternative had to be considered.

Bill Vardy was also handy with metalworking so offered to make a "thunder box" for the Toyboys. He got together some timber and Colourbond sheeting and before you know it they had a loo that any outback cattle station would be proud to have. It was a caravan type system and installed in the courtyard for easy access. Problem number one solved.

Problem number two. It had a storage tank which had to be emptied from time to time by taking it away to a disposal area. Luckily John Boulton had experience with caravans and a similar disposal system. The Toyboys unanimously agreed to volunteer John for the job. Problem solved!

Socialising also improved as all together, they were able to take a morning "smoko" and have a bit of a chat. These morning meets were also an opportunity to discuss on a casual basis various aspects of their operations.

It was no time to rest on their laurels though, toys had to be made. The next Children's Festival was coming up and they had to make sure they had plenty of the give-a-way toys. It was all systems go to also ensure that there was a good supply of other toys to be able to sell at the Festival.

The recipients of toys this year were;

- Grace Manna House
- Meadow springs Education Centre
- The Parents Place
- Downs Syndrome WA
- Esther Foundation
- Peel Health Foundation
- Make-A-Wish

Bill Vardy again! He had been pretty busy in his own shed turning out some terrific items. He made a very special rocking horse out of an Asian wood called jellaton. You could not only cut it easily but you can carve it. The horse was made without any particular donor in mind but it was finally decided to donate it to Peel Health for a fund raiser towards Downs Syndrome. I believe the amount paid by the highest bidder was $2,100.

Another job well done

YEAR 2012

We received a cry for help from a very caring mum who had a vision impaired son. She wanted to give him some independence with washing has hands or helping at the kitchen bench.

The Toyboys did not hesitate and got straight on to it. They made steps with a rail and wide steps for easy balance. It was a joy to see the smile on his face. This is what the Toyboys are all about.

Toy Boys make son's day

I WOULD like to extend a very big thank you to the Kim's Toy Boys.

I found Kim's Toy *Mandurah Mail* and decided to call them and ask if they could make a couple of wooden things for me.

I needed them to be strong and sturdy for my 23-month-old son who is vision impaired.

Although my son has a disability I like him to still be as independent as possible.

The Kim's Toy Boys made the stool with steps small enough for my son to climb up by himself.

They also put a rail on it from the bottom to the top so he can hold on while getting up and down and made the top step a nice big platform ably and be able to turn around.

I couldn't have asked for anything better.

They made it just as I had wanted and more.

And to top it all off they did it all free of charge because of my son's disability.

They were very happy to help and put in the extra effort which is very hard to find these days.

I just want them to know how much I appreciate what they did for my son. Thank you again.

Ashlea Byrne
Greenfields

YEAR 2013

CHAPTER 25

There must have been something in the air this year as there was a surge in guys wanting to join the Shed.

Dennis Eacott was originally a mechanic and then progressed to be a planner and buyer in the mechanics bay at ALCOA (there for 39 years). When he retired Dennis and Norma got the wanderlust so off they went for the next few years travelling seeing Australia and the world (definitely no caravans says Norma).

Dennis had his own shed and enjoyed making the bigger type toys. A big doll's house for his daughter, a sit on Thomas the Tank for his grandson, and so on.

He met Lew Hanna through basketball and Apex, and Lew suggested he join the Men's Shed. He did that and before you know it, he was part of the team.

Unfortunately, a few bouts in hospital kept him away from the Shed from time to time, but it was a comforting thought to him to know that when he was feeling OK he could go to the shed for a bit of camaraderie and feel useful making toys.

Kevin Baxter was an aircraft engineer who put in his time with the Navy, TAA, MMA and Ansett. (I bet there are a few stories to tell there). He bought a farm in Bridgetown and was self-sufficient until it all fell apart and he moved to Mandurah to retire.

He had done woodworking at school and liked "fiddling around" with wood things at home. Not sure where, but he got hold of the Men's Shed number and spoke with John Boulton. After an "in-depth interview" John said "Well, if you think you can get along with everybody, OK". He was in.

He fitted right in and enjoyed producing all the different types of toys. When asked to make a new type of toy, or copy one we did not have, he found it very satisfying to be able to make it happen.

Not being one of the youngest at the Shed, he said "I'm getting on a bit now, so am slowing down. I am happy to just help other boys with their projects".

John Templeman was originally from Northam where he was a welder. He moved to Mandurah and started a mobile welding business which he ran until he retired. He met John Boulton through Scott Park Homes and became friends. They both enjoyed early morning rides on their bikes.

John B spoke to John T about The Men's Shed and suggested it would be worthwhile him joining. He had to really think about it, as the Toyboys didn't make metal toys where he could use welding. His woodworking skills basically ranged from nil to zero.

He threw caution to the wind and said "Let's do it". He started helping Paul Ellis with the doll houses and credited Paul with teaching him woodworking. While never a "star" he became quite adept at producing some of the smaller toys. It helped that he used to go to Paul's home shed and get some extra tuition. He can't praise Paul enough for the patience he showed and the skills he passed on.

Said John "I enjoyed the fellowship the Shed provided and was proud to be part of such a community minded bunch". He left the Shed in 2019.

Dave Smith was the Manager of Peel Tyre Service until he had a severe stroke after heart surgery in 2011. It left him partially incapacitated and took some time to be able to function, albeit limited. While attending a session at the Head Injury Unit, they suggested he approach the Mandurah Men's Shed as part of their charter was men's welfare.

That sounded okay but as a woodworker he made a good chef. He went and had a chat though, and despite that, he became part of the fold. John Boulton became his mentor and took him under his wing.

Being a quick learner he was soon able to help others with toys being made. He and John became a team working on some of the large special projects that groups such as the Events Team for the City of Mandurah wanted made. His big benefit to the shed was that he learnt where everything was. You needed 15mm nails for the nail gun. Ask Dave. You couldn't find a certain router bit. Ask Dave. Having a guy like Dave at the Shed is gold.

"I am thankful that such a friendly outlet was available to me. You can take the piss out of someone and they don't take it to heart" said Dave.

Allan Lewis was a butcher (again an occupation – not a Kim relative) and had a food manufacturing business in Bentley. He sold out in 2007 and went into retirement. In 2011 he and Beverley built a house in Mandurah and moved there. During this period he was involved with motorbike racing and help build and repair them with family and friends (he is still a bit of a petrol head).

While on an overseas trip in 2013 Allan met a fellow who was a member of the Australind Men's Shed. He had never heard of Men's Sheds but the idea of it appealed to him. As soon as he got home he looked up the Shed in Mandurah and called John Boulton. He visited the shed, liked what he saw and joined up.

Like so many who joined, he only had basic woodworking skills. He had done a furniture making course and a picture framing course at TAFE, but that was about it. Allan remembers that his first task was helping Lew Hanna make dolls cots. From there he progressed to being able to work alone and now is quite adept at producing some pretty fancy work.

He believes that the members are not only proud of being part of a community minded group, but it gives them an interest in life. Some members have their own shed but you can only make just so many things for the home.

"They can now start a job at the Shed and finish it off at home" he commented.

CHAPTER 26

The High School decided to celebrate the 50th Anniversary of Dr. Who, by having a photo session with students dressing up as the Doctor. To help make the day a winner, the school asked the Toyboys if they could make a Dr. Who TARDIS, Dalek and K9. After a bit of head scratching John Boulton and Bill Vardy decided they could make them. This was the result...

TARDIS

Dr WHO books & photos

YEAR 2013

Dalek

K9

As the group was growing in numbers it was discussed and agreed that meetings should be restricted to a managing committee of office holders and committee members. At the Annual General Meeting the first committee was elected as:

    President– John Boulton
    Vice President – Graeme Gordon
    Secretary/Treasurer – Irene Boulton
    Committee –Jack Williams
            David Smith
            Bill Vardy
            Kim Butcher
            Colin Baker
            Ken Green from the Doghouse Club was invited to attend.

The first order of business to attend to was how many giveaway toys would be needed at the Children's Festival. A figure of 1,500 was decided on so it was noses to the grindstone. The usual stock of toys for sale was also required so another busy year was coming up.

FROM TOY BOYS TO SHED MEN

The Halls Head Community School presented Kim with a pair of sneakers they had decorated, as part of their project "Our Island To You World", which focused on Kim's Toyboys. Alas, nobody knows where they have vanished to.

The City of Mandurah approached the Toyboys regarding a proposed competition for kids at this year's Children's Festival. They wanted a sit-in wooden biplane, which they named Red Bessie. To enter the competition children had to follow Red Bessie's "flight path" in a lead-up to the festival as she made special appearances at different locations throughout the city.

Entrants had to submit a photo of them sitting in Red Bessie and answer the question:

"If you could fly, where would you fly to and who would you take with you?".

The competition winner was five year old Willem Pepper who said;

"I would be Peter Pan and I would take my grandfather Captain Pepper, a pilot who died in his Lancaster plane in the war".

Willem was over the moon winning Red Bessie and could not wait to get her home to invite his school mates around to play.

Looking to the sky

FIVE-YEAR-OLD Mandurah resident Willem Pepper has an airline legacy he is proud to look up to.

His grandfather Captain William Pepper was a Royal Australian Air Force Association pilot in World War II, flying Lancaster aircrafts and leading a crew of seven.

Sky's the limit: Five-year-old Willem Pepper with his Red Bessie.

How's that for happy?

There is a volunteer group called the Mandurah Muscateers Charity Computers who repair and/or recondition used computers and laptops. These items are donated to community groups and third world schools in overseas countries. They also sell some, at a very modest price, to underprivileged people.

They approached the Toyboys to see if we could help with new shelving and work benches. No trouble to us we said. Before you know it, we had them all done and installed. They were very appreciative and offered to help us if we ever needed help with computers in the future.

Apart from what was mentioned with the Festival, the following groups received a donation of toys;

- Meadow Springs Primary School
- Supporting Our Seniors
- Peel Health Foundation
- Make_A_Wish
- Zonta Club
- North Mandurah Primary School
- Downs Syndrome WA
- Heartkids WA
- Esther Foundation

YEAR 2014

CHAPTER 27

Bruce Bailey was the school principal at Coodanup College when he gave it away in 2012. He then just tinkered around at home doing odd jobs to keep himself busy.

One day he walked into Bunnings and Kim' Toyboys were there showing how they made children's toys. This looked interesting so he took one of their cards.

As he was always into woodworking (mainly making home furniture) he gave John Boulton a call and arranged a meeting. He liked the setup the group had so he started in August 2014. He enjoyed being able to learn from the more experienced boys and improved on his "home woodworking" skills.

When asked what sticks in his mind with the group, his reply was "I loved sitting at our morning break and hearing the stories the boys had to tell".

Bruce left the Shed in 2020 due to an illness but is still likes to keep in touch.

Half way through the year the Shed was hit with a bit of a shock. A new member enquiry was being made. From a woman!!!! Goodness gracious me, what is the world coming to?

Lesley Williamson had a friend who bought one of Paul Ellis's wooden models. He loved the workmanship, but not being into woodworking himself suggested to Lesley that she approach the Men's Shed about joining.

She was a non-working mum who did the school runs and tinkered a bit with minor repairs around the home. So she said to herself "Why not?". Called into the Shed, had a chat and before you know it, was one of the "boys".

Contrary to what some might think, she was welcomed into the group. She had no airs and graces and fitted right in. Wasn't above being able to relate a slightly off colour joke. The toys she made were of a very high standard. Her personal pride would not let he produce anything that was not top notch.

Lesley became part of a sub-committee looking at the quality of toys produced, but she became the main "quality controller". If she didn't think finished jobs were not quite up to scratch she would tactfully get the maker the fix it or even fix it herself.

She enrolled in University and at the end of 2019 qualified as a registered nurse. Her first posting was in early 2020 so that put a finish to her Shed work. She remembers the Shed as a place where everyone was welcome and ready to give a hand when needed. When asked to sum up her time at the shed she replied "I gained some good friends".

Ray Wright was a carpenter until health issues forced him into retirement.

He was at loose ends and was looking for something to keep himself occupied. As Irene Boulton is his sister, she suggested he joins Kim's Toyboys. That sounded good to Ray so John took him along to have a look. It suited him as long as he didn't have to do anything strenuous.

Ray took on the job of cutting out the wheels that were used in the give-a-way toys at the Children's Festival. Some think this is a tedious job, but Ray was happy to plod away and contribute his bit.

He would have turned out a couple of thousand wheels until ill health saw him give the Shed away in late 2017.

This bumped our numbers up to 14 members.

CHAPTER 28

Bill Vardy made a model of a hard rock special Mining Shovel for Boddington Gold. They were going to raffle it at function to raise funds for Children's Cancer Research. The company took one look at it and said – no way! We are going to keep it for our office – here is $5,000 towards the raffle proceeds. It is now housed in a glass case in their front office.

There were a few subtle suggestions by some members that additional machinery and machinery replacement parts would make life a little easier with jobs. The committee saw that their funds position was fairly healthy so agreed to consider it.

A check of the working areas showed that there was enough room to accommodate more machinery but additional power points would have to be installed. As the college had no objections to this, new power points were arranged and suppliers contacted to supply machinery, parts and tools. There were now some very happy chappies.

It should be mentioned how generous Bunnings are with community groups. John Boulton was the nominated person to liaise with Bunnings and as he lived in Erskine he dealt with the Halls Head branch. The contact at the Halls Head store was Mandy and she was a delight to work with. They provided the Toyboys with dressed timber to the value of about $300 each three months. This may not seem a lot to some people, but the boys were very grateful.

The affiliation with WA Men's Sheds was showing a few hiccups as the National body was requiring operational changes that did not sit well with Kim's Toyboys. A sub-committee was appointed to investigate and report back. The results will be recorded at a later date.

The Esther Foundation requested that a dolls house be made available to them as they were having a fund raising auction soon. As they had been given other toys in the past it was agreed that the one Paul had just finished would be provided. The winning bid was $2,300.

YEAR 2014

Diversity South is a not-for-profit organisation that helps people with a disability to have some sort of independence. They approached the Shed and asked if a young man named Tommy Stelmach could come along to the shed one morning a week. He had the basic use of his hands so we agreed to have him cutting out wheels and gluing one wheel to an axle ready for the Children's Festival. He was thrilled to be able to do this and gets into it with gusto.

A short while later they asked if another young man named Josh Barton could also be helped. Josh was in a wheelchair but had reasonable use of his hands. He too was accepted and was teamed up with Tommy also making wheels and gluing axles. They are both delightful young men and enjoy the morning breaks with the members. Some ribbing is given to them from time to time and they accept this as being all a bit of fun.

The AGM this year returned the same members to the committee but with Bruce Bailey added to it.

The Children's Festival once again blessed us with fine weather and a great attendance made it a most successful day, not only by giving away nearly 2,000 small toys, but financially.

Children's Festival workers

Later in the year Lesley Williamson saw that there was no promotion of the toys that were for sale. Her suggestion was that we be on Facebook and volunteered to set it up. By the end of the year it was up and running with photos of the toys we had available.

Now there were orders for toys coming through and even some special project requests. She became the "controller" and responded to people making contact for orders or special requests. It is interesting to see the different items people want made out of wood (some we can, some we can't).

Before closing for the Xmas break, the committee decided to have all members carry out a big clean-up and the culling of unwanted old timber. It was to be followed by a barbecue lunch. This was a good move as it brought together members from all working days. For quite a few it was the first time they had met one another, as they worked on different days.

It proved to be a good morale booster and was made a standard function in future years.

Records were a bit patchy, but here are some that received donations from us;

- Wandering St John's Ambulance
- Zonta Club
- Rotary Club
- Esther Foundation
- Make-A-Wish
- Three Day Care Centres

YEAR 2015

CHAPTER 29

It looked like being a very lean year for new members but then late in the year one popped up.

Brian Allison was the General Manager of the WA's largest transport refrigeration company, Thermo King, before he retired. Thinking he might like to work part-time he and Carol moved to Adelaide for four years where he worked in the casino and sports clubs.

Back in WA he had a heart attack in 2013 and had a stent implanted. He recovered well but had a hard time accepting it mentally and became a bit reclusive. His doctor recognised this and recommended he look up the Men's Shed as they were said to be about men's wellbeing.

He looked them up and spoke to John Boulton who invited him to the Children's Festival where they had a stand. He did that, had a talk and John invited him to come in on Tuesday at the Shed to have a look, and talk with the boys to see if they were compatible. He must have been because he started on Thursday.

When asked about woodworking experience he said "When I was 5 years old I had a photo taken with other kids pretending to cut wood. That's my only experience". Graeme Gordon took him under his wing and taught him the finer points of toy making. He must have been a good teacher, as Brian turns out some pretty fancy work these days.

In his first week he was conned into bringing cakes as the "new boy". He did that but then was told "Oh no, we meant for the first year". He did that for a while until he realised he had been had. In fact, he still often brings in his home made cakes.

He summed the Shed as "It is an enlightening experience. It is true what they say – Men's Sheds are there to help with general health and wellbeing of men".

CHAPTER 30

One of the rewarding parts of dealing with community groups is the number of nice people you meet. Because they are community minded their hearts are in the right place and they just want to give. Two such people are Christine and Shirley from Make-A-Wish. Kim's Toyboys, and then the Men's Shed, have been supporting Make-A-Wish for many years, dealing with the "terrible twins".

They will just drop in, full of cheek, and see what we able to do for them. However, sometimes it is just to drop off some "surplus" materials, such as timber or paint that they have happened to come across. They have become some of the Shed's favourite people (it helps that Shirley sometimes brings a bag of homemade Rocky Road). Ya gotta love 'em.

One day the girls called in and said they needed our help with a fund raising idea. They had a bag full of motor vehicle badges and asked if we could make dartboard case incorporating the badges. It would then be part of their next fund raising auction. Anything for these girls. The boys got to work and within two weeks came up with this masterpiece. The feedback was that the case was a very popular item at the auction with the "rev heads".

It was certainly something different

The Southern Districts Volunteer Fire Brigade is like all community groups, funding is always a problem. They approached the Toyboys to donate something for their auction. Rather than give a toy from stock, it was decided to do something special. The outcome was a scale model of a fire truck, which alone raised $1,800 at the auction.

How good is that?

YEAR 2015

The weather was kind to us for this year's Children's Festival. The rotunda was now our standard spot and people were filing through all day. At times there were four lines, six deep with kids wanting to glue wheels on a toy. It was all stops out for the Toyboys, but it was so satisfying to see the smiles on those kids' faces.

The type of toy kids could choose

Busy at the rotunda

Although a relatively new boy, Bruce Bailey was asked to complete an application to the City Council for a grant as he had experience in completing various applications with the Education Department.

The City Council made available to community and charity groups, from what they called their Partnership Fund, monies for the continuance of the volunteer operations. He was not only happy to do it, but the result was a whopping $11,700 grant payable over three years. Good things do happen to good people.

Bunnings approached us to see if we would hold a woodworking session at their Halls Head store. There would be two trestles and some material provided and we could show children how we make some of the toys.

This was a great opportunity to showcase the Shed and people to see what we do. Five of our members participated and were kept busy during the three hours we were there.

A box of the small toys we usually give away at the Children's Festival was taken along and we soon had a steady line of kids gluing the wheels on the toys. They could not believe it that when they had finished the gluing, they could keep the toy for free. That got a big tick for the Shed.

At the Annual General Meeting the newly elected committee was;

> Chairman: John Boulton
> Deputy Chairman: Graeme Gordon
> Secretary/Treasurer: Irene Boulton
> Committee members: Bruce Bailey, David Smith, Bill Vardy, Jack Williams, Kim Butcher

This may not be all, but it is only what I could find from records available. Toys donated this year were to;

> Give-a-ways at the Children's Festival (about 2,000)
> Make-A-Wish
> Manjimup Education Support Centre
> Zonta Club
> Friends of Peel Hospital

YEAR 2016

CHAPTER 31

2016 was a popular year with eight new blokes joining the Shed. This was helped by the committee deciding to add Wednesday to the mornings the Shed was open. It now made it easier to spread the load of workers over three days. Each member was restricted however, to attending on two days only.

Don Masters had a busy life from running a general store in Byford to travelling around Australia with his wife and three kids. Then back in WA as a carpenter with the Public Works Department in the North West. Even as a deckie on a boat for a while.

He retired to Mandurah in 2014 and kept busy with handyman type woodworking around home. He described himself as a basic woodworker but felt that one day he might like to hone those skills.

His chance came at the Mandurah Children's Festival in 2015. He called into the Mandurah Man's Shed display and had a chat with John Boulton. John said they were looking for new members and told him to come to the Shed after Xmas. Don was the "first cab off the rank" in 2016.

He found that the members were "good blokes" and he felt comfortable settling in. They were patient in showing him the finer points of toy making. He progressed very well and was soon turning out toys like the best of them.

"One good lesson I learnt was to be more patient in finishing off a task" he said.

Don is well remembered for being the only member to ride his bicycle to the Shed. Rain, hail or shine he peddled his bike in to the courtyard and propped it up in his little spot. He did cop a few comments about being "Flash Gordon" but it was all in good humour.

Graeme Kuypers worked at the ALCOA mine sites as a "time and motion" man and then later as a TA and gopher as he puts it. When he retired from there he and Karen jumped into their caravan and set off over east. Their main target was NSW to see his mum, as that is where he was originally from.

He had some woodworking experience and had this crazy idea of making a wooden clock. He found a "grumpy old man" named Cliff Dibney who was a so-called wooden clock expert. Cliff was able to give him some good pointers.

Graeme made a timber framed mirror for his daughter and it turned out so well he decided to make a few and sell them at a "wood market". This was good move as he made a few dollars. Looking for somewhere with a bit of mateship he approached Kim's Toyboys but they were full. He went to Falcon Men's Shed but they too were full. So he went back to making more mirrors and made a few more dollars.

12 months later he again approached the Mandurah Men's Shed and this time was told "Come and have a talk with the boys and if you get on okay you can stay". He stayed.

Graeme liked the variety of toys that were being made and was soon in the swing of things. One comment was 'It is a good learning place. I found there was an easier way of doing many of the tasks".

He is also the resident expert on beekeeping - especially on bee stings.

Norm Taylor qualified as a cabinet maker but worked most of his time as a contract carpenter. He had his own shed for not only woodworking, but he did some spray-painting and mechanical work. At one stage he bought a speedway car which he did up.

On retiring he didn't do much other than a bit of fishing. His wife Jeanette was still working so he called himself the "kitchen bitch". His daughter got on his back and told him that he should get out more - find an interest.

So he tracked down a number for the Mandurah Men's Shed and spoke to Irene Boulton. She pointed him in the right direction and he checked out the shed. John showed him the setup and said there was one more spot available on a Wednesday. He was in.

He made some toys but his preference was in making children's furniture. His specialty became making kid's tables in varying sizes to suit different ages. This did not stop him from tackling other jobs as needed. He is concerned though that that sometimes workers do not put enough priority on safety measures.

Norm says it is one of the best decisions he has ever made. .After putting in a morning at the Shed he leaves the place feeling good. His thoughts about the toys we sell are "We sell them too cheap. But what can you do, that's what we are all about isn't it?"

FROM TOY BOYS TO SHED MEN

Barry Ash had his own Business Consultancy and was an Auditor. When he retired he decided he would join a men's shed as he had renovated houses and was making furniture items at home.

Our old friend Dr. Google came good with a contact number for the Mandurah Men's Shed so he gave it a ring. He arranged a meeting with John Boulton and starting cutting timber there the next week.

Barry never specialized in any particular type of toy, just happy to work on the next type required. He had special thanks for Kevin Manning who was very helpful in settling him in and helping to improve his woodworking skills.

When asked to sum up his time in the Shed he simply said "Fantastic". Barry left the Shed to help out in his son's business in 2020.

Phil Bingham grew up in the wheat belt and worked as a mechanic. He left there in 1990 and moved to Pinjarra, working in the mines as a mechanic, and then later as an operator (not a Smooth One he says). Itchy feet got him and Julie the travel bug and started travelling to all parts of Australia. Progressing from a camper van to a caravan this continued on through his retirement in 2014.

After retirement they moved to Mandurah and he enjoyed his handyman jobs working in his shed. Unfortunately, they ended up next door to the neighbour from hell who had a firewood supply business. The noise of wood cutting was constant day and night. To save his sanity Phil looked for an interest that would take him away from that for short breaks.

It took him a while but finally found where the Men's Shed was. He called in, knocked on the gate, and was given a tour. Everything clicked so he started that week. It didn't take long for him to settle in and was soon an important part of the team.

"I enjoy the companionship and the jovial attitude of most of the guys. It also helps to take break up the monotony that everyday living can sometimes give" he commented.

If you want to know about Men's Sheds Phil is your man. Every September he goes on a "crop inspection tour" in the country. Every town he comes to during their caravan trip he looks up the local Men's Shed and has a nosey.

Brian Tillet Had an eclectic working life. Was a truck driver for Fremantle Port Authority for many years, was a Postie and had his own party hire business. He retired in 2013 and spent a lot of time fishing from both beach and jetties. He didn't elaborate on any "fishing" stories but we can imagine.

Brian was experienced in woodworking having made a lot of kid's toys and most of their own home furniture. They moved to Mandurah and he felt joining a Men's Shed would be a good move for him. He had his own Triton Workbench but wanted to be able to use different machinery to make things.

He approached the Falcon Shed first but they were very small and seemed to be more interested in him paying rather than being welcoming. Undaunted, he then called in to the Mandurah Shed and had a talk with John. John was on a roll with new members coming in so offered him a place with the Wednesday group, which Brian accepted.

He did not specialise in making any type of toy, as long as it rolled forward or went up and down he made it. He just wanted to make toys that entertained kids. The constant production of toys and the enjoyable company suited him down to the ground.

"I particularly enjoy the "smoko" break. The banter around the table can get rather interesting" Brian said.

Bill Love was a cook (not a chef he says) for the British Merchant Service and then the Australian Merchant Navy. When he retired he took a fill-in job as a cook at the UWA student accommodation which turned into being ten years.

He finally moved to Mandurah in 2009 and did volunteer work at the local soup kitchen.

There was an article in the local newspaper about the Mandurah Men's Shed and he thought that might be something that could interest him. So he called in one day to the Shed and had a chat. Knew very little about woodworking apart from a course he took on wood-turning years ago.

The result was he signed on and started learning. He admits there were a few disasters at first but he stuck to his guns and after a while was able to produce work that he described as "acceptable". Under the tutorage of Jack Williams he concentrated on the cut-out toys that were given away at the Children's Festival.

Bill enjoyed the camaraderie and friendliness that the Shed gave him. Unfortunately he had to resign from the Shed in 2020 due to ill health. He said "Being there was a great experience and if it wasn't for these aches and pains, I would still be there".

Syd Ness grew up on a mixed produce farm in Port Lincoln until it was sold in 1982. Then caravanned for a while, had a deli in Busselton and finally back in Adelaide taking on a lawn mowing round. The franchisor asked him to set up the franchise in Perth which he did. Syd managed this, including his own round, until 2013 when he semi-retired. He still cuts a few lawns each week to keep busy, which is not bad at 87 years of age.

His wife and daughter encouraged him to get out more and mingle. So he joined the National Servicemen's Association and Mandurah People Who Care group, which he still does some volunteer driving for every week. This was fine but his daughter thought he might need something more productive. She visited the Mandurah Men's Shed stall at the Greenfields Children's Day where she picked up John Boulton's business card, gave it to Dad and said "Why don't you try them?".

Syd had some basic carpentry skills picked up from his farming days, so he rang John and started there one morning a week which progressed to two mornings a week later on. His first job was making a kiddie wheelbarrow. It was a bit tricky with all the angles but he got there. After that he made any toy requested of him, but preferred the bigger items like kid's furniture.

He has never regretted joining the Shed as he now mingles with "a great mob of blokes". "I thoroughly enjoy the yarns that are spun at the morning break" he added.

The Shed numbers are gradually increasing with the count now being 23 members.

CHAPTER 32

Paul Ellis is our master craftsman in making dolls houses. In fact, he is the only member who makes these detailed ones. His main aim was to make a special one as first prize for the raffle we held each year at the Children's Festival. He also made a few others for sale or as items at community group fund raising auctions. The problem was, they were too popular as more and more were asking for them. It became necessary to start spreading them out as we couldn't help everybody.

Some of the dolls houses

FROM TOY BOYS TO SHED MEN

The old problem of quality control raised its head again. There were too many toys being put into stock that needed a bit of a touch up. The boys got a slap on the wrist and it was stressed to them the importance of having quality toys being available to the public.

Apart from the huge influx of new members, 2016 was a significant time in our history.

Graeme Gordon advised the group that there was an increasing movement of Men's Sheds in Western Australia. Men's Sheds have been in country towns for many years and there was a gradual increase of Men's Sheds in metropolitan areas. There was an existing Shed in Falcon but not one covering the Mandurah catchment.

There were well over 100 Sheds throughout WA and a state office had been established with a State Government grant. The state operation offered benefits to its members of administration assistance, exchange of ideas, insurance connections, zone meetings and much more. There was a membership fee applicable but it was not very much.

Graeme was concerned that another operation may open as a Mandurah Men's Shed and detract from what Kim's Toyboys had established. He recommended therefore that Kim's Toyboys change their name to Mandurah Men's Shed. The initial reaction was "shock" and discussions on the suggestion were held with all members. The main concern was the loss of the Toyboys name as a huge amount of time, effort and heart had gone into building up a reputation. Kim was very proud of his "boys" and would be sad to see that recognition go.

The longer established members were most concerned that the Toyboys name would no longer be recognised. They had weathered the good times and the bad times and were an integral part of what Kim's Toyboys were all about. But, they could also see the benefits that being part of the Men's Shed movement would bring them.

They were stuck between a rock and a hard place. Logically changing the name would be of a benefit, but emotionally it was hard to agree to lose their well-known name. There was no pressure on anybody to make a quick decision as this was a momentous time if it was to happen.

After several meetings with the members a compromise was agree upon. All agreed to vote in favour of the name change, but wherever possible the wording "Formerly Kim's Toyboys" would be used in promotional material.

A Special General Meeting of members was called and on 26th May 2016 a motion was passed to change the name Kim's Toyboys Inc. to Mandurah Men's Shed Inc.

A new era of operation was now to start, flying a new flag.

With the Change of name we applied for and were accepted as a member of the Men's Shed Association of WA. Our members were now able to enjoy the benefits they provided.

As the scribe of this tome I am going to use poetic license to give a personal opinion on one aspect of the state operation that gets to me. When notices are sent out by the state office they refer to the members as "shedders". This conjures up in my mind a picture of hair being shed all over the place and constantly being swept up by bald headed men. Or perhaps dandruff being continually brushed off shoulders.

Again, just my opinion so let's get on with the story.

The recipients of toys this year were;

    Grace Manna House
    Meadow springs Education Centre
    The Parents Place
    Downs Syndrome WA
    Esther Foundation
    Peel Health Foundation

Patron thanks Men's Shed for toy contribution

Mandurah Men's Shed patron and local MP David Templeman thanked the members of the group at a morning tea at their premises at John Tonkin College in Tindale Street

Mr Templeman said the 40 members of the group had this year made over 3,000 wooden toys which had been distributed to Children in Care, local needy families, playgroups, community groups and local festive events.

"These magnificent members of our community love what they do, they enjoy the friendship and camaraderie that comes from coming together ach week to make these toys and our community benefits hugely from their generosity" he said.

Mr Templeman said that there were now 15 Men's Sheds in the Peel region and they were an important community network for those involved, plus they were a great outlet for blokes to gather with other blokes.

"I am so proud of this group, that was started a number of years ago by Kim Butcher and a few mates who would gather regularly in is back shed and has grown into what it is today" he said.

Mr Templeman said that the Men's Shed members were now firm fixtures at many community vents and festivals, particularly at the annual city of Mandurah Children's Festival, an event that sees them inundated with kids and their families and where they, this year, handed out over 2,000 wooden toys to visitors to their stall.

YEAR 2017

CHAPTER 33

This year saw **Stan Schleisher** join our bunch. He was originally a carpenter but progressed to a stage where he owned and operated his own building company.

He also had a flying license and tinkered with a British Dehaviland Chipmunk plane that he had for 30 years. When he retired he bought and renovated a "North American Texan" an air force training plane

After that he was at loose ends so a friend suggested he find a Men's Shed.

Being a sprightly 82 years old he felt he still had plenty to give. He popped in one day to our Shed, had a talk and has been there ever since.

Stan doesn't claim to be a dynamo as he just plods away turning out toys at his own pace. He said "I am like the tortoise, slow and easy wins the day".

Rod Napier had been an electrician all his working life up until the time he retired.

Looking to keep himself busy he approached the Men's Shed to see what they were all about. When he found out they made wooden toys he was a bit hesitant as his woodworking skills were very basic.

It was suggested by John that his electrician status would be most valuable in repairing and maintaining the machinery. This suited him fine, so he started there and even managed to make a few toys.

Rod was at the Shed until 2020 when he resigned due to ill health.

CHAPTER 34

Kim's health meant that he wasn't out and about as much so he didn't visit the Shed often these days. Still, he liked to know what was going on, so popped in for a chat occasionally and check up on his "boys". His mind however was still as sharp as a tack.

You can't keep a good man down

FROM TOY BOYS TO SHED MEN

There was an approach made to the John Tonkin College by a women's group to use the Shed facilities on a Monday. This created a dilemma for both the College and ourselves. The first consideration of course was discrimination if we were to say no to the approach. The next thing to consider was the use of machinery and tools.

The women's group had neither and expected to use ours. Our insurance only covered members and they did not want to become members as they wanted to make their own things and not toys. It would appear this was only a tester for us as the group never pursued the matter and it died away.

There were some disagreements with the National Men's Shed Association and some of the state bodies. It centred on the national Board make up and state funding. Three of the states pulled out of the national scene and for some legal reason our state changed its name to simply Men's Sheds of WA

The Annual General Meeting this year was a fairly quiet affair with only a few items discussed. The main ones were how the change of name would affect coming operations and confirmation that we would not be charging membership fees even though other Men's Sheds do.

Office bearers stayed the same with the new committee being:

Bill Vardy, David Smith, Jack Williams, Dennis Eacott, Bruce Bailey, Colin Baker

A sub-committee for toy quality control was appointed, being:

Colin Baker, Lesley Williamson, Jack Baker, Paul Ellis and. Kevin Manning

Toys given away at the Children's Festival were again a big success. Just over 1,100 wheels on toys were given to smiling faces.

It is all about the kids

YEAR 2018

CHAPTER 35

Kevin Atkins. February saw my retired life say goodbye. I joined the Men's Shed.

My background was through finance, the real estate industry and with TAFE as a lecturer (real estate). I had met Graeme Gordon through Rotary and he introduced me to the Shed. I had always been a "desk jockey" but my Dad taught me the finer points of woodworking. My projects were usually wooden furniture or fittings for the house.

We discussed my experience with woodworking as a hobby and he felt that I should fit right in. I had always known about Men's Sheds being throughout WA and had it in the back of my mind that it was the sort of thing I would be interested in once I retired.

I still say that Graeme had an ulterior motive for bringing me in. They wanted a person to take over the secretarial side of operations and he knew I had experience in that area.

It is a very demanding position and takes up a fair amount if my time. As I say, "At least it keeps me off the streets". Don't get me wrong, I thoroughly enjoy doing it.

David Matthew started a garden lighting business that he built up and then took to Melbourne. He eventually sold the business in 2015 and moved back to Perth.

David says that woodworking was taught to him by his grandfather in Kalgoorlie. The interesting thing though, is that his grandfather was virtually blind. Despite that, he was able to work efficiently in his workshop. David was in awe of the workshop as he says there was an unbelievable amount of tools and machinery.

Although the house that he and Sabina bought was new they wanted some changes, so David spent the next few years doing additions and renovations. Once that was behind him, he decided he needed to join a group where he could improve his woodworking. He too tried the Falcon Men's Shed and was curtly told "We're full and there is no waiting list".

With his tail between his legs, he went online and was able to find a number for John Boulton. A totally different reception as John said "Come on in and we will see what you look like". He must of looked OK as he started there the following Wednesday.

He is happy to have a go at any task he is given and has had some interesting ones. "Being at the Shed is a lot of fun due to the sense of humour of the guys" he said.

"The Shed is just what I wanted to do, as it is a marvellous institution that helps give meaning to life' he added.

Kevin van der Burg was the mobile equipment workshop supervisor at ALCOA until he retired in 2013. He was getting under the feet of his wife Bernice who "quietly" suggested he find himself an outside interest. Golf sounded good so he gave it a try. Like all golfers, it soon became his addiction. Kevin still plays at least two days a week.

After some caravan trips and golf games he felt he would like to do something a little more productive. He had read about men's sheds in the newspapers but could not find contact details for a Mandurah one. Finally the Shire came good with John Boulton's number and he made contact.

Kevin started attending one morning a week and he too progressed to two mornings. He well remembers his first task. John gave him a set of plans for a train and carriages and said "Have a go at that. If it turns out OK you can take it home". He ended up making more of the trains to put in stock.

After that he was happy to turn out any toys that were required. Kevin was often given the job of completing a special request item which he enjoyed doing. His crowning glory was making a giant deck chair for Mandurah Tourism with just a photograph and basic sizes to go by. He's pretty proud of that.

"My joining the Shed provided me with the relief from boredom not mixing with like-minded people" he said.

Noel Pitcher originally trained as a shipwright but later qualified as a cabinet maker. He worked for a number of years with a company making and installing screens, doors, window treatments etc. He "sort of" retired in 2000 and ran a cabinet making business on a part time basis.

He moved to Mandurah in 2007 and kept busy with a bit of cabinet making and as a volunteer with the Salvation Army. He was looking for something a bit more challenging, preferably mixing with other men. Noel heard that a group of men were making toys at the High School so he called in one day and had a talk with John. They seem to like one another and he started there on the following Wednesday.

You might call Noel the quiet achiever as he plods away at his bench. Happy to make what might be required but prefers the mid sizes toys rather than small ones. He is impressed with the amount of tools and machinery that a Shed has, which makes woodworking that much easier.

Said Noel, "They are a good bunch of blokes, and the Shed keeps me out of mischief for at least one day a week".

Allen McLeod was originally from New Zealand where he apprenticed as a cabinet maker. He moved to WA and worked as carpenter on mine sites in Paraburdoo, Tom Price and Laverton. He then ran his own commercial aluminium business until he retired.

Now living in a unit in Mandurah he no longer had his own shed to work in. He didn't actually get the shakes but he did miss not being able to do something other than tend the small garden he and Elizabeth have.

Allen is not sure where, but he heard somewhere that there was a group working out of the John Tonkin College. A phone call to the college put him in touch with John who told him to call in and talk to the Wednesday supervisor and see what you can work out. This he did, worked things out and started straight away.

He prefers working on toys with a difference. Something from a plan that he has to give a bit of thought to is right up his alley. Other than that, he likes to make the bigger toys like kiddie's prams. He is well entrenched now and enjoys the camaraderie and the ability to talk to others about men's issues.

"The Shed is not only well designed to cater for men's mental health, but it stands for the community at large" he commented.

Harry Butler is the Operations Manager of boat lifting at the Mandurah Marina but also has his own wood turning business. He turns out some marvellous pens, trophies, bowls etc. He is a member of the Wood Turners Association and has submitted some great items at their "Turnfests". His latest effort is a miniature eggcup, goblet and wine bottle which, wait for it – they all fit at the same time on a five cent piece. The mind boggles.

Harry had been a friend of the Shed for some time and called in from time to time with timber he had come across. He decided it was about time he became an official member and did so this year. He has been a great help in showing members techniques in wood turning.

He is a strong advocate of the Shed and is happy to contribute with "odds and sods", as he puts it, to help with any items being made for a charity group. We tend to go through a fair few band saw blades and Harry has taken on the job of repairing them.

He only attends one morning a week but said "It is good to see old blokes and learn new tricks".

CHAPTER 36

I had only been attending the Shed for a few weeks when John Boulton came to me and said he had a request from a man to make his grandson a toy car storage rack. The man wanted it to hold about 100 Matchbox toys and look like a road train. John gave the job to me and said "There you are Kev, show us what you can do". This really was a bit daunting for me, but I got stuck into it and the granddad was tickled pink with the result.

The Shed comes good again

It was our first Shed day in July when John Boulton arrived with the crushing news that our Mentor and great friend Kim Butcher had passed away. There was a sombre air with the Shed for a while with members recounting the times of Kim. A strong contingent from the Shed was at his funeral to farewell him. There is no doubt that if there are big Sheds in the sky, Kim's will be the biggest and best run of them all.

The state government decided in their wisdom that all clubs, not-for-profit organisations and community groups should register with the Department of Mines, Industry Regulation and Safety (formerly Department of Commerce) a copy of their Rules of Association (e.g. Constitution). The registration was to be completed on-line and included annual trading figures and auditors certificate.

It was at this stage that Irene Boulton gave notice that she would not be re-nominating for the positions of Secretary and Treasurer. She did not feel confident of being able to complete all the government regulations required and preferred for it to be handled by someone with applicable experience. This was a blow to the Shed as she was a valuable cog in the big wheel of the Mandurah Men's Shed. Not only did she keep good records of the Shed's operations, but she was a big part of the behind the scenes activities. If anything, she spoiled the boys as she was always there to pick up after them if they slacked off. After ten years in the two positions she was definitely going to be missed.

A little while after Irene dropped this bombshell Graeme Gordon came up to me and casually said "Kev, how would you feel about coming on the committee?" The "committee" turned out to be the Secretary/Treasurer position. I am not saying nobody else wanted the job, but I did get appointed unopposed.

It was to be a challenging position as new Government regulations were coming in and members had to comply with the changes. This didn't sit too well with some members as they felt the "old ways" were better. It did create some anxious moments, but we got through it in the end.

Graeme Gordon won the job of putting together our new Rules of Association (herein called Rules). Men's Sheds of WA had a "model rules" document that was to be the starting point as one for our Shed. Some adjustments were made and the finished product was presented to the Members at a Special General Meeting in August. The document ran to 30 pages, so I feel it was a case of "too hard" and not many of the members actually read it. There were some feelings of "If it ain't broke why fix it?" The simple answer was that Big Brother says we have to.

Despite that, there was unanimous agreement at the meeting and the necessary paperwork was lodged with the Department. As with most government paperwork if you don't dot the i's and cross the t's you get it back. Sure enough we did too and had to amend bits and pieces. Well, back to the drawing board.

As we had to re-do the form it was decided to amend some areas that we felt would improve the Rules. The wording was done, accepted by the members and the form re-lodged. This time it was accepted. That is not the end of though, there has to be an annual return lodged following every AGM.

The AGM was held on the same day as the Special General Meeting and the main item of general business was about the upcoming Children's Festival. Everything went to plan for attendance at the Festival but unfortunately the weather was against us on the day and it kept people away. I guess you can't win them all.

Seeing as he did a good job with his last effort, Bruce Bailey was nominated to lodge an application for a grant with the City of Mandurah.

The election of committee members resulted in;

Chairman – John Boulton

Deputy Chairman – Graeme Gordon

Secretary/Treasurer – Kevin Atkins

Committee – Denis Eacott, David Smith, Jack Williams, Bill Vardy, Paul Ellis, Colin Baker, Ken Green, Bruce Bailey, Winston Rennick.

A suggestion was put to the members that the Mandurah Men's Shed should have its own branding and logo. Two layouts were put forward with the noticeable thing being dropping the wording "formerly Kim's Toyboys".

This did not sit well with some of the more long standing members as Kim's Toyboys had been an important part of their lives. The majority of members voted to change the branding, but with the "train" staying as part of it.

Once again we saw operations flying under a new flag.

There were some thoughts that we should perhaps investigate the possibility of securing our own premises. While the use of college premises was most favourable to us, there is no guarantee that it will last forever. All committee members were asked to give the matter consideration but nothing concrete ever came of it.

Three of the committee attended the opening of the new Cockburn Men's Shed to see what $1.3million will get you. We were a long way from that.

With the change in branding, Bendigo Bank was approached to sponsor, and pay for, new shirts for our members, which they agreed to do. All we had to do was agree on a colour. A choice was given to members of bone, grey or light blue. A vote was taken with all members and grey won in a photo finish from blue.

As some new members leave the Shed after a short while (for a variety of reasons) it was agreed that a new member could only receive a shirt after being at the Shed for three months.

David, Don and Phil sport the new shirts

The situation with the Doghouse Club was raised in relation to insurance. They felt that by attending on a Friday they were members and covered under our insurance. This was shown to not be the case and they were requested to complete formal membership applications.

There were only five people who continued on as members of the Shed. They were Ken Green, Winston Rennick, Julie Park, Rhonda Dilworth and Robert Paul. This changed the Friday attendance in as much as any new member could now be allocated a Friday, and all had to comply with the Rules. This included the making of toys for distribution.

Men's Sheds were gaining a reputation of being somewhere that people could approach for minor jobs they needed done. In particular it was the elderly, physically handicapped people, community groups, jobs too small for a business to handle or people with no manual skills whatsoever.

There were many requests that were beyond our expertise, but some that come to mind that we were able to help with were:

> A chairman's gavel.
> Mah-jong boards.
> A 750mm timber circle for a table top.
> An archway for a school ball attendees.
> Repair an arm for an antique chair.
> Cut out birds for a children's activity..
> Cut-out leaves for a school project.
> A "bi-plane" shelf.
> Medal presentation trays for Police and Emergency Services Games

The donating of toys continued with recipients being;

> Friends of Peel Health
> Make –A-Wish
> Lifeline
> Mandurah Primary school
> Amana Living (Wearne House)
> Treasured Tots Day Care
> Elipsy Purple Day
> Zonta Club

YEAR 2019

CHAPTER 37

This year saw a big surge in new membership. There was no particular area from where they came; it just seemed that the reputation of the Shed was becoming more widely known.

Paul Pickett did not have a specific trade but was an odd-job man who could turn his hand to many things. He did like woodworking which he learnt from his dad as a youngster.

He had at one time approached the Forrestfield Men's Shed but found the reception a little cool. He moved to Mandurah shortly after that where his wife Angela joined the Mum's Cottage craft group. The husband of one of the ladies used to have an association with the Mandurah Men's Shed and gave Angela info about it.

When Paul called in to the Mandurah Men's Shed, the reception was just the opposite of the other Shed. After having a chat with John and myself, he was keen to join up and started one morning a week. He thoroughly enjoys tackling any job that is allocated to him.

He says the Shed is a wonderful institution where volunteers can give something to the community. "Men can also get together to enjoy some fellowship and develop friendships" he added.

Eric Baker had a signwriting/advertising/screen printing business in Bayswater prior to retiring. He and Barbara had a holiday home in Mandurah and eventually moved down there. Retirement saw him helping out their kids with house renovations, their businesses and so on. If that wasn't enough, he was a volunteer at the Rail Historical Society in Bassendean for a while. They still found time to go caravanning which is one of their great pleasures.

Eric enjoys his golf and it was there he met Graeme Gordon. Graeme had often spoken about the Shed and what they do. Eric thought this might be something that would suit him. He had some experience with wood work at his business, and making some home furniture. His own shed was also fairly well decked out with gear.

He called into the Shed giving Graeme as a referee and was shown around. Eric was very impressed with the set up and toys that the guys were making. Convinced, he started there the following week.

Eric was happy to work on any task he was given, even cutting out the 1,000 little round circles for a City Council event. So far he has made some of the smaller toys but said he would like to tackle something a bit more intricate.

About the Shed he said "I enjoy the morning breaks and listening to the various characters expounding about world affairs".

Bob Fitzgerald had 22 years going around the world with the army, and ended up in Canberra. With bad luck and bushfires they had two houses burnt down there, so he and Mary moved to WA where they had family.

He went into a partnership supplying and installing heaters, skylights, gas heaters and solar systems until he retired. Bob described himself as "bush carpenter' but thought he would like to find an avenue where he could improve his skills.

Bob became a volunteer at Vinnies where he met Winston Rennick. He found out that Winston happened to be a committee member of the Mandurah Men's Shed and arranged to go and have a talk with them. He liked what he saw and joined the Shed in July.

He feels his woodworking skills have picked up and the other members have helped him to knock a few rough edges off his work. When asked about his time in the Shed his reply was "All the guys are friendly and make me feel like part of the organisation. I feel at home".

Kevin Geeves was a jeweller in Brisbane and ran his own business before retiring early this year. He and Christine then moved to Mandurah where they had family. While attending church services he kept his ear out for any talk about community organisations as he wanted to join a fellowship group.

The name Mandurah Men's Shed cropped up and as he had heard of Men's Sheds in Brisbane as being for good community contact, thought this may be the one. One problem though, he knew nothing about woodworking but thought it was an opportunity to learn something new.. He wandered down to the Shed and the first person he saw was me. He said he was keen to learn a new skill so we started him in the Friday session.

He was partnered with Allen McLeod who showed him the basics of woodworking. He was a keen learner and was grateful for the patience and kindness the members showed to him. Slowly but surely he is getting there. When asked about his settling in, he said "It was very pleasing to be accepted in to the Shed without any previous woodworking experience. The guys were not judgemental, they are good people".

(Would you believe it, we now had five Kevins attending at the Shed).

Don Peterkin was originally an installer of long distance radio links working for electronic companies. He then worked as a contractor installing antennas and radio equipment for oil drilling companies. On retirement he has buried himself in his "complete" workshop, fiddling around as he puts it.

His first effort at woodworking was when he was 21 years old. He saw a "Danish Deluxe Lounge" in a magazine and thought "I can make one of them". Someone had given him some teak wood planks from an old pilot boat in Albany. With this and some more he bought he ended up with a very presentable lounge. He got the bug, and has been making things ever since.

Don describes himself as a home body but felt he would like some company with "old blokes" who were like minded. He had known about Men's Sheds and tracked down where the Mandurah one was. After calling in one day, having a talk and a look around he put in an application to join.

He finds it most commendable that there is a group of men who produce toys for charitable groups and underprivileged families. When asked about his contribution to it all he replied "I am just an old fart who likes making a few things".

Colin Purcell was a Duntroon Army graduate who served in Vietnam in 1970/71. After 21 years he had done his bit and left the Army. One later job he had was with the Department of Commerce and Trade. His job was to promote West Australian food and wine travelling to Asia and South Africa. What a job!! As he says "It's was a tough job but someone had to do it".

Colin knew Winston Rennick from church and Vinnies. Winston suggested to Colin that he might enjoy attending at the Men's Shed . Colin was a basic woodworker and had done a bit of DIY projects at home. He said he would give it some thought which he did for TWO YEARS. He figured that was enough time thinking about it and finally made application to join and started attending on Fridays.

He is very impressed with the work that the Shed produces, whether it is for community groups or special projects. One comment he made was "I am amazed at the type and variety of machinery the Shed has to work with. We are well placed to turn out any job".

Phil Barbagiovanni immigrated to Australia from Italy in 1960. He was a carpenter/joiner and got a few jobs here and there. Finally he got a permanent job with Main Roads working on bridges and roads. You might call him a steady type, as he was with them for 47 years until he retired.

Retirement saw him gardening, working in his veggie patch, a bit of fishing and maybe odd carpentry jobs for friends. His wife Francesca said he spent too much time around the house and urged him to find an outside interest.

He knew of Men's Sheds so checked out what was available. Mandurah looked promising so he called in and had a talk with John. Although he was recovering from a shoulder operation, he was given a start on making the smaller toys for the Children's Festival.

Phil is a bit if a quiet achiever and plods away at the job he is given. He likes what the Shed does as it is not for profit and provides an avenue for older men to have in outside interest in life. He doesn't mind making the small toys but admits "I would like to use my learnt skills on some bigger projects". He might be sorry he said that when the next tricky special project request comes in!

Geoff Winton is a mechanical designer and project manager who is in semi-retirement. He takes on projects from time to time but likes to tinker around in his shed. He has made things like furniture and kiddies desks but not so much small toys.

He knew of Men's Sheds and felt it would be the perfect place to mix with people and learn new woodworking skills. Geoff is involved with Rotary and spoke to Graeme Gordon about the possibility of joining. Graeme referred him to me.

Talking with him, he said he not only wanted to improve his skills but he might be able to use his mechanical designing to create new toys for the Shed. It sounded like a win-win situation so we signed him up.

It was late in the year and before he could start was offered a contract in New Zealand which would take him away for a few months. We won't be seeing him now until 2020.

Norm Jones came from a dairy farming family and helped run the dairy until it was sold when he was 37. After that he got a job with the Education Department as a gardener firstly in Point Peron and then Broome. When he left the Department he and his wife bought and ran chalets in Denmark. Finally retired to Binningup where he was a part-time gardener at the Country Club.

After a spell of travelling they moved to Mandurah but shortly after he became a widower. His friends urged him to join a men's shed as he had built up his woodworking skills while running the Denmark chalets. After a bit of searching he finally found the Mandurah Shed and popped in and had a chat with me.

Norm liked what he saw and shortly after started attending one day a week on a Wednesday. He is not a pushy type but is gradually getting to know the other guys and enjoying the camaraderie.

He feels proud to be part of a group that is doing so much to help underprivileged families and support community groups. He made the comment "I feel as though I am achieving something by producing toys that will be appreciated".

Our popularity is increasing with member numbers now standing at 39.

CHAPTER 38

Legislation woes again raised its ugly head. When the Rules were registered the Department deemed that as we received some donations the Shed needed to hold a Charitable Collectors License. More paper work. This time the task fell to me, which included arranging police clearances for three nominated committee persons and an up-to-date auditors report. As a result of this requirement we now had Ernest (Ernie) Gobby officially appointed as our Auditor.

Thankfully, the application was passed after a list of requirements was satisfied and we were now licensed. This meant another annual return to be lodged. Will the red tape never stop?

There was some concern that members were becoming lax in cleaning up after themselves at the end of a session. Tools not put away, unfinished jobs on benches, wood shavings on machines and so on. This was being unfair to the next day's men who came in. A strong message was given to all members that they had to mend their ways and work as team members. It was taken to heart and things did improve.

The college advised us that they were putting some students in various places of work to give them experience of a working environment. They were put in a place based on their thoughts on where they might like to be employed in a profession or trade.

We agreed to accept a young boy one day a week for a period of ten weeks. This was a new experience for our men as some of them now became tutors. I am pleased to say that both our guys and the young lad came out unscathed. In fact when the lad gave his final report to the college he gave a glowing account of his treatment by us and the amount he had learnt.

Graeme Gordon became ill and resigned the position of Deputy Chairman. He stayed as a member as he was determined to beat the problem and get back "in the saddle" as soon as possible. Allan Lewis was appointed to fill the vacant committee position but a new Deputy would not be appointed until the next AGM.

This year we had our first marquee at the Rotary Club Family Fun Day (commonly called the Rotary Duck Race). It was not as successful as the Children's Festival but we could see where improvements could be made at future events. However kids still managed to put wheels on over 500 free toys. It was arranged that at the next Rotary day we would refer kids with their new free toy to the Rotary Club booth where they could paint it.

Ready for business at the Duck Race

It was pointed out that the two physically impaired boys Josh and Tommy were not covered by our insurance if they had an accident at the Shed. The solution was that we make them both members, which we did. Their Carers were OK as they were covered by other insurances.

There was a problem with our mail from time to time with our address being at the college. The college has two campuses (or is that campi?) and our mail sat for weeks if it was delivered to the Greenfields campus. The solution was to have our own Post Office Box address which we did. Our official mailing address was now **P.O. Box 4101, MANDURAH NORTH 6210.**

I raised with the committee the situation that the recording of operations was being done on the computer of whoever is Secretary. This did not sit well with me as I believed it should be centralised. It was suggested we contact the Muscateers Computers who we had helped in the past, to see what could be done. I trotted off, had a chat with them, and they were more than happy to help. They donated to us a laptop with all the trimmings. This made life much easier, as being mobile the laptop could be taken to meetings if necessary and best of all, passed on to future Secretaries to use with all past records intact.

Following on from this I figured I was on a roll and suggested we now move further into the twenty first century and look at having our own email address. There was some hesitation as to the ongoing cost it would create. However, Winston said he

YEAR 2019

could set one up at no cost to the Shed. This he did, and before you know it we now had the email address of mandurahmshed@gmail.com. All of this seemed so easy I nearly suggested we get our own mobile telephone number but did not want to push my luck. Maybe next time!

Allan Lewis was keen for the Shed to consider buying a covered trailer and obtained a quote from Mandurah Trailers to build one. A trailer could be used for transporting toys to and from Festivals, collecting donated timber, delivering donated toys or even using it as a pop-up sales outlet. The quote was for $10,300 and it was decided that an application would be made to Lotterywest for a grant of $9,000 for us to be able to buy it. Lotterywest advised that applications take about four months to process so we had to keep our fingers crossed until the New Year.

Every year Passages Youth Engagement Hub have this weird event called the "Lounge Chair Race" where young guys race old lounge chairs with wheels on them down the street. Once more we were asked to come and attach the wheels to lounge chairs. Is there no end to the variety of skills our members can demonstrate?

There were murmurings among the members that the toilet we had, had gone past it's used by date and we should look at something a bit more up-market. The search began and we finally agreed on a top of the line job. As the cost was around $4,000 it was decided to apply for a grant from ALCOA to fund it. This was done but we were advised that the processing of grants could take some months, so we paid for it from Shed funds in the meantime. When it was installed the boys could not believe how spoilt they now were.

Out with the old!

In with the new!

FROM TOY BOYS TO SHED MEN

At the AGM the new committee was elected as follows;

>   Chairperson – John Boulton
>   Deputy Chairperson – Allan Lewis
>   Secretary/Treasurer – Kevin Atkins
>   Committee; Norm Taylor, Bill Vardy, Dave Smith, Lew Hanna, Ken Green and Winston Rennick

The Shed was once again represented at the Children's Festival and this year the weather was most kind to us. Our stand had a steady stream of parents, kids and grandparents coming through. The sale of toys, raffle and donations brought us in just over $4,000. The main event, of course, was the gluing of wheels on to give-away toys for the kids. There were only a handful of those toys left after we gave away nearly 1,600 toys on the day.

Raffle 1st prize

Raffle 2nd prize

It was quite evident that we could have sold a lot more toys if we had EFTPOS facilities. The committee had been hesitant to install it in the past as it was considered that the associated costs were too high. I did some investigation and found a system called "Square" that I felt would be suitable. The machine cost $59, would fit in the palm of your hand, it ran off a mobile phone and ongoing costs were just 1.9% of each transaction. The committee could only say yes. We now had EFTPOS. The shed was slowly catching up with the technological world.

We have a very good relationship with the Events Team at the City of Mandurah. They are a delightful bunch of young ladies and they look after us well when it comes to our spot at the Children's Festival. Every now and again they want a little job done and will approach us for it to be completed.

This time they said they had a Xmas tree on which they wanted to hang stars and circles. The idea was that children could write their name and a small message on them and then hang them on the tree. We said sure and asked how many they wanted. "A 1,000 of each would be nice" was their reply.

We didn't exactly faint but did rock back on our heels a bit. Our recovery was fairly quick, and we agreed to help out. They are so nice it was hard to say no. Eric Baker was given the job of cutting out 1,000 circles and I was to do the stars. It took a while but we got there. Isn't that what we are there for?

I had been made the go-between for Bunnings so I opted to deal with the Greenfields store as it was closer to the Shed. While trying to wangle some timber from them, my contact, Hayley, asked if we could make a Father Xmas chair if they supplied the timber.

With all the help they had given us in the past, there was no hesitation and we said yes. The job was given to the dynamic duo of John Boulton and Dave Smith. The result was a throne fit for a king and Bunnings were delighted.

You can't have Xmas without Santa

FROM TOY BOYS TO SHED MEN

They say there is no such thing as a free lunch. The Men's Shed had been enjoying the use of the John Tonkin College work rooms at no cost and we were very grateful for it. This was to come to a sudden halt. The Education Department advised that from the 1st January 2020 we would have to pay an annual rental for using the facilities. The amount was set at a massive $150 per annum. It was decided not to set up special crowd funding to cover it, petty cash was there if need be.

The "Visit Mandurah" office, which is the local Tourist Bureau, contacted us to see if we could make a special tourist attraction for them. They provided us with a photo and basic dimensions of a giant Adirondack garden chair. It was to be placed on the foreshore near the well-known big Moreton Bay fig tree. Now, that was a challenge. The task was given to Kevin van der Burg and he did a marvellous job. As soon as it was installed, the feedback was that it was an immediate hit with snap happy overseas tourists.

MANDURAH'S BIG DECK CHAIR
A giant deck chair is the latest attraction on Mandurah's eastern foreshore and another step in Visit Mandurah's vision to make the city more attractive to Instagrammers and other social media users. The local tourism organisation commissioned the Mandurah Men's Shed to make the chair, which now sits in a prime position overlooking the estuary with Mandurah's famous Moreton Bay fig tree as the perfect Instagram backdrop. Visit Mandurah General Manager, Anita Kane says the local Men's Shed was a joy to deal with. "It's a fantastic organisation and I hope we can work together again in the future," she says. The Mandurah Men's Shed welcomes inquiries: mandurahmshed@gmail.com

Anita Kane, Norm Taylor, Kevin Atkins, John Boulton, Kevin van der Burg and Allan Lewis.

YEAR 2019

Just before we closed for the Xmas break, the college gave us a notice that all members of the Shed had to obtain a Nationally Coordinated Criminal History Check to be able to work on school property. This caused some consternation as they would not accept the usual Police Clearance or Working With Children Card that some members held.

To make matters worse the new clearance could only be applied for on-line and some members did not have a computer. It had to be finalised before the college resumed in February next year so it gave everybody nearly two months to sort it out.

Toy making was progressing well and we donated toys as follows:

- Dwellingup P&C Association
- Rotary Club of Mandurah Districts
- Make-A-Wish
- Ruggers Junior Football Club
- Foster Share Shed
- 5 Play School Centres
- Pathways Spiritualist Church
- John Tonkin College
- Mandurah Primary School

YEAR 2020

CHAPTER 39

Despite the turmoil of COVID 19 and the reduced hours, there was still some interest in people wanting to join the Shed.

Peter Donovan spent 20 years working in submarines with the British Navy and then the Australian Navy before deciding he should be a "land lubber". This experience won him jobs in the maintenance area of mining sites and refineries. His last job before retiring was with BP Oil Refinery. His job as Maintenance Supervisor was to ensure that *"they keep that thar oil flowing".*

His woodworking skills were learnt by watching his father and picking up pointers. His projects were mainly with home furniture items – shelving, kid's tables etc. He grew to love this pastime albeit with a very basic work area and tools supply. He described himself as a "frustrated chippie".

Peter was aware of the Men's Shed operations and felt that this is where he should go if he was to improve his skills with woodworking machinery. Once again Dr Google was consulted and it showed a few Men's Sheds in the area. As our Shed was closer to his home he contacted us.

He settled in well and is happy producing some of the toys we give away at Festivals. Once he is more at home in the Shed he hopes to produce a few toys for his grandkids. He did add "This is an opportunity for me to chat with other men and provide a little break from domestic life".

John Lysaght spent a number of years working for a company that retailed computer supplies and stationery. With this experience, he started his own company which he had for twelve years.

Now retired, he moved to Mandurah. Lawn bowls was his game so he soon found a club he could join. This was great but he felt he needed more outlets to keep him busy. As he had dabbled a bit in the past with woodworking he thought it might be the thing.

He converted half his garage to a workshop and started to build up a woodworking operation. To help with his skills he did a woodworking course in Dwellingup that entailed making furniture. He said "That was the best thing that I could have done. I was amazed at just what I could produce."

Gradually, he built up his tools and machinery and was able to make some impressive wood products. The use of the machinery however was a bit noisy for the neighbours (an anonymous note in his letterbox was a clue). This made him look at where he might be able to continue woodworking away from his home.

Google once again gave directions to our Shed and he called in for a chat. It all worked out well and he started straight away. While he was happy to start on some of the toy production, he felt more comfortable making larger items. This worked out well for the Shed as we were looking to step up the production of children's furniture.

John commented that "I am not sure what my final niche is going to be in retirement, maybe it's with the Men's Shed".

CHAPTER 40

We were back hard at work when one of the members came in and declared "The chair is gone". He was referring to the giant garden chair we made for the Tourist Bureau. There were several theories put forward as to what might have happened, with some unflattering ones about Mandurah inhabitants.

A phone call was made to our contact at the Bureau and we got the real story. The Crab Fest was coming up and the licensed drinking area was next to the chair. The City Council was concerned that some over anxious drinkers might get up to antics on it and cause themselves an injury. It was to be replaced after the Crab Fest.

I would like to tell you a delightful story that happened just because of us being a Men's Shed. Late in 2019 a mum contacted me and asked if her son's school could get some wooden offcuts for the kids to carry out a project of "making" wooden objects. We provided her with a bag of bits and pieces and she was very grateful.

January this year she contacted me and said "My goodness we have created a monster, my son Jamieson won't stop making wooden things. He loved working with wood on the project so much he just wanted to keep going". He now has his own workbench, all sorts of woodworking tools and is now trying to convince his parents that he needs a jigsaw.

Future Shed Man???

Jamieson hard at work and the finished product

Good news! Lotterywest came good with the grant so we could now go ahead and get a covered trailer made.

Early in the year there was a disastrous series of bushfires in the Eastern States that destroyed many homes. Not only homes but there were a number of Men's Sheds totally destroyed. All that hard work of building up machinery, tools, fittings and materials – all gone. To say the least, the Shed Men were totally devastated.

The Kalamunda Men's Shed put out an urgent call to all WA Men's Sheds to see if they could donate any surplus materials they had that could be sent send over east. Kalamunda was prepared to coordinate and collect what was available and ship it over east.

We were able to contribute some machinery, tools and support materials which were enough to fill a trailer. The response was overwhelming from all sheds in WA and finally two semi-trailers of supplies were sent east to give them a kick start.

The Rules of Association were still creating a few hiccups with shed operations. Some could still not come to grips that the Rules were a legal requirement and had to be complied with.

I was given the task of identifying any areas in the Rules that could be amended, without being contrary to The Act that would help smooth the waters for the future. There were nine areas that I felt could be tweaked to make life easier. These were put to a special meeting of members and thankfully they were passed. Here's hoping this will be the last of it.

A bubbly lady named Kerry from the Performing Arts Centre (PAC) popped in to see if we could make a dog for use as a children's activity. Not just any old dog though, it was to be 120 centre meters tall, be on a mobile stand and covered in chicken wire. The idea was that kids would tie small strips of material all over it so it would end up looking like a shaggy dog. To sweeten the deal, Kerry brought in a couple of batches of homemade cakes. How could we refuse?

The job was given to the dynamic duo and after a lot of to-ing and fro-ing the final result had Kerry jumping up and down and hugging everybody. I think she liked it!

PAC put it on display during the school holidays and the kids had a great time tying the material strips on it. Kerry said she was tickled pink with the result.

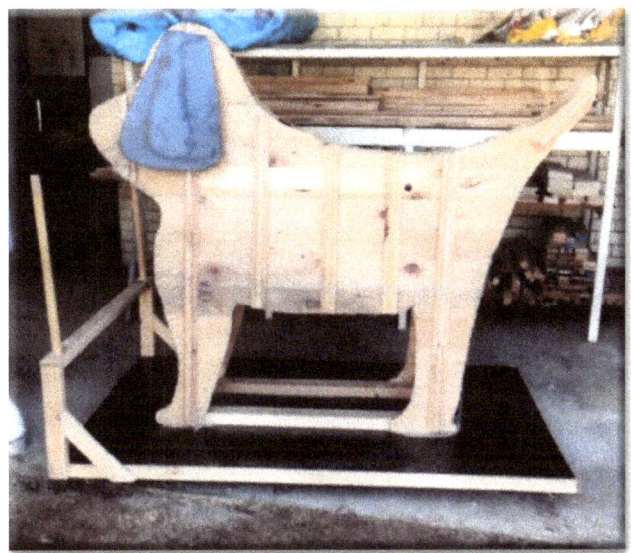
Big Dog ready for his coat

His new shaggy coat

It is a bit of a downer when a happy story has to be followed by a negative report. The requirement that we all get a National Criminal Clearance took some time for members to get it all in place. Unfortunately, for varying reasons, we lost seven members as they were not returning to the Shed because of the hassle with the clearance requirement.

Those who had Police Clearances and/or Working With Children Certificates, still had to get the extra one and they thought this was an imposition and gave it all away. This has been a disappointment to the Shed as we are now without some very experienced workers.

If that was not bad enough, a depressing event followed soon after.

Early in the year a strain of flu emanated from China. Due to the ease of international travel it quickly spread throughout the world and became an epidemic. Hundreds of thousands were affected and many thousands died from it. The World Health Organisation declared it to be pandemic. Australia reacted by introducing drastic measures to try and contain it.

Non-Australians were stopped from entering the country. People were banned from meeting in groups of more than 100. Sporting events were held without any spectators. Workers were encouraged to work from home if possible. Businesses were closing, staff being laid off and parents keeping their children away from school. These measures were like none that had been seen for 100 years.

In mid-March The Western Australian Department of Health issued guidelines for the hygienic practices in the workforce. They were extremely detailed in the actions that had to be taken, and the limited contact that should be between workers. The type of work that was carried out at the Men's Shed made it impracticable to impose those restrictions.

Added to this was the fact that the members were in the age group who were most susceptible to catching the virus.

The Shed committee decided that the Shed should close down for at least 4 weeks after which a revision would take place. This was a big disappointment to some members as this was their major interest away from home. Most of members however agreed that it was the right step to take as the protection of member's health was paramount.

It is eerie to know that the day after our decision to close the Shed was made; the Government announced that there was to be the closure of all hotels, pubs, clubs, restaurants, cafes, churches and group gatherings. It is almost that we had a foreboding to close before being ordered to do so.

Only venues with take-a-way food and essential services could continue to operate. The general public was urged to stay in their home unless they had an essential need such as food shopping or medical assistance. The streets, although not totally deserted, were taking on wartime like appearances.

The journey of the Shed was suddenly at a standstill. How long these dire times would last was anybody's guess. Some members have their own workshop and were able to keep their hand in. Others, such as those living in units, did not have that "luxury" so have to tough it out until they can return to their sanctuary of the Shed.

Although I write this part of the story in the present tense (mid-March 2020), I am actually only a part way documenting the history. It was easier to report these events as they happened rather than rely on memory later on (got to be careful about old-timers disease). The only positive aspect is that because I am self-isolated for goodness knows how long, I have more time to work on this anecdotal masterpiece

So, keep tuned in for the next instalment, being when the Shed is able to re-open the doors.

CHAPTER 41

It is three months since we had to close the Shed due to the coronavirus. This gave me a lot more time to work on this journey with the result being that I am now writing in real time. From now on (mid-June) I will be recording achievements, events, people or whatever, as things unfold.

During our enforced COVID 19 isolation (the Big Sleep someone called it) the Shed lost one of its valuable assets. Due to a personal situation, John Boulton resigned as Chairman and then as a member of the Mandurah Men's Shed. This was a terrible blow as he would be a hard person to replace.

It was not fully appreciated how much work he did for the Shed. His woodworking skills and knowledge of support materials was just one aspect. He worked tirelessly behind the scenes to ensure that the operations of the Shed worked as smoothly as possible. It will be interesting to see who can fill those big boots.

Just when we thought we were happy campers' itching to get back to our home away from home, along comes news that dampens the spirits. The college advised that new rules are that community groups can no longer have use of college facilities while children are in attendance at the college. This effectively meant that we could not have access to the Shed until 3.30pm on weekdays. As it is likely that the finish time will be 6.00pm it creates a couple of problems. One, that gives only 2 ½ hours working time and two, it is too close to meal time for many members.

Some members said that this is unworkable for them so they will stop attending at the Shed. To be sure we keep all the current members the question has to be asked "Do we start once again to look for other premises?"

In addition to this, the college is arranging for a risk assessment audit to be done of our rooms and Shed operations. It will cover areas such as electrical points to machinery, woodworking dust, timber storage etc. We dread to think what this might turn up. Oh – happy days!

The audit has been completed and was not as bad as we thought it would be. The main issues were timber and items stored above head height, use of extension cords and dust control. A member's working bee is to be organised to rectify it all so they can get back working in the Shed.

The working bee took place and what a week it was. "We'll knock it off in a couple of days" says I. Boy, was I wrong. Scads of old timber had to be thrown out to make way for the usable timber stored too high and had to be put on lower shelves. Tins and boxes of bits and pieces from deceased estates that were donated to us were not really re-usable, so out they went. Old tools that were beyond repair – out they went. The more we got into it the more we realised what hoarders we were. If something hadn't been used in eight years, was not salvageable or not of use on our operations – out it went.

We had to be realistic and accept that a lot of the gear we had was donated second hand. It was great that people thought of the Shed when they had unwanted tools or timber (e.g. deceased estate). If we are honest though, a lot of it was unusable but it was difficult to say no to them. Consequently we ended up with cupboards of bits and pieces that we would never, or couldn't, use. It was a case of bite the bullet and "clean house" with a vengeance.

All of this resulted in the filling of two skip bins. In addition to this, we also took two ute loads of old paint to the recycling depot. All in all it was a job well done by the guys and resulted in the college agreeing to let the members back in the following week.

As it was school holidays we were able to have the boys back in at the normal times for a week. It was a bit disappointing that only half the usual numbers turned up. A lot of them were still smarting from being relegated to late afternoon times. A fair number of the members have already told me that they will not be attending the Shed at the new afternoon times. Their hope is that we find a new home so they can return to the fold.

CHAPTER 42

With the new attendance times it is almost like a new era of Shed operations. The new times have seen a drastic drop in the number of members who attend at the shed. Weekdays (3.30pm to 6.00pm) has seen between 3 and 7 people attend each day, which is well down from 15 to 20 that has been the norm. A Saturday time has now been added from 7.30am to 12noon, and this saw 8 attend.

We do have some members not attending because they are away on trips or have health problems, but 50% have indicated that they will not be returning to the Shed until better times can be arranged. This will undoubtedly have an effect on future production of toys. We now have less people working less hours, therefore the numbers say – problems.

But, enough of this negativity – let's get back on the positive track.

How's this for positive – we have our new trailer! It looks a bit swish and just needs to have the interior fit out done by our boys. It is planned to use it as a "pop-up" sales outlet at events in and around Mandurah so we can sell toys. This will be essential as the annual Children's Festival, where we always sell a lot of toys, has been cancelled because of the COVID 19. There's no keeping us bad boys down.

It is said that it is a small world, and I am a definite believer. I recently went on a short holiday to Broome with my wife Debbie, my daughter and her husband. Being the first time in Broome we naturally had to do the touristy things. We went on a small boat down the river among the mangroves, and on board there was only our family and one other couple. Half way through the trip my daughter called out to me "Dad, didn't you have something to do with Toyboys in Mandurah? This chap here says he did too". He came over to me and introduced himself – Eric Rawlinson.

I couldn't believe it and blurted out "Bloody hell I've been looking for you for 6 months". He looked a bit nonplussed, until I explained I was looking for early Kim's Toyboys to help me fill in gaps with the writing of this journey. He then told me that Peter Addi-

Our new toy

son, another early Kim's Toyboy, was his father-in-law. We agreed to catch up once we were both back in Mandurah and have a chat about his days with Kim's Toyboys. Fancy having to travel 2,000km for a chance meeting with an old Toyboy. What are the odds?

He is not Superman or the Caped Crusader, but David Templeman MLA is a hero as far as the members of Mandurah Men's Shed are concerned. He has been a strong advocate of the Shed over many years and once again he has gone to bat for us. When we told him about the reduced hours at the Shed, he approached the College and was able to negotiate better times.

These will now be 9.30am to 2.15pm on weekdays. Thank you David, you are a lifesaver (that screaming you can hear in the background is our members rejoicing).

Hold up Boys! There is a proviso. There is a door leading to a college walkway that will have to be bolted from their side so we cannot have access to school grounds while schoolchildren are there. So far the college has involved a Safety Inspector, a Site Engineer, a Building Inspector, the Fire Brigade and the Education Department Head Office to okay a bolt being fitted.

Five weeks, and still no indication as to when we can take up the new times. Talk about using a sledge hammer to crack eggs. Unfortunately, all we can do is wait for all the red tape to be dealt with.

YEAR 2020

Last March we had a request from Good Start Learning Centre in Meadow Springs to build them a "street library". Unfortunately COVID 19 struck and we had to close down. We had been back in business for two weeks and they contacted us to ask if it could now proceed. Our answer was yes.

Unbeknown to us the Centre had a fund raising drive selling "cookie dough"? For every one sold they received a part of the sale price. Because of their structure they had to nominate a non-profit community group to receive the proceeds, and they nominated our Shed.

Last week Regina from the Centre sent me a note telling us that they had finished the drive and had sent- wait for it- $784 through to our account. How good is that? It just goes to show that good deeds do sometimes get rewarded.

The library has now been delivered to the Day Care centre and the staff were quick to fill it with books.

Happy Librarians?

It was suggested that in order to attract donations and help obtain grants, we should apply to the Government for endorsement as a "Deductible Gift Recipient (DGR)". This meant that any person/organisation providing or donating funds to us can claim the amount as a taxation deduction. However, it transpired that before we can be approved we need to be classified as a "Charity". So, off we go and lodge that application and now we are officially a Charity. Back we go to the DGR application lodgement to finally get approval. Let's hope that all this work will attract some funds.

But wait, there's more! (No, not steak knives). While all this processing was going on a very helpful lady at the Tax Office pointed out to me that as an incorporated body we are obliged to lodge tax returns. She did say however, that we could apply for tax exemption as we were a not-for-profit charity. This was promptly done, and I thought I would trust my luck and threw in a request for GST exemption as well.

I know we knock the Government for all the red tape requirements but I must say that the Tax Office have been most co-operative and helpful. In fact, the exemption applications were back approved in a week and we are now Tax exempt and have a GST concession.

Our AGM rolled around again with only a small change to the committee;

>Chairman – Allan Lewis
>Deputy Chairman – Graeme Gordon
>Secretary/Treasurer – Kevin Atkins
>Committee – David Smith, Ken Green, Allen McLeod, Winston Rennick and Bob Fitzgerald.

At the AGM certificates were issued to recognise those who had served the Shed for more than ten years. Every one of these people was instrumental in fostering Kim's Toyboys, and then Mandurah Men's Shed, to help make it the success it is today.

10 Years

Brent Taylor – 2000 to 2010
Barry Beament – 2001 to 2011
Rudy Goh – 2009 to 2020
Irene Boulton – 2008 to 2018

15 Years

Graeme Gordon – 2003 to present
Colin Baker – 2003 to present
John Boulton – 2003 to 2020
Jack Williams – 2005 to 2019

20 years

Paul Ellis – 2000 to present

The COVID 19 shut down and then our restricted attendance hours, made it harder to keep up with toy production and special orders. Full marks however to our boys as they had heads down and bums up feverishly working away.

One special order came from the Foster Share Shed which is a local community group that supports foster parents with clothing, recreational items and activities. They had donated to their Shed a large collection of Matchbox toys but did not have a suitable container that they could store them in.

That prompted a call from them to the Mandurah Men's Shed to build a storage container that could easily be rolled away each night. You may recall that early in this journey I made a wall rack for such toys so it was thought that it was just a case of adapting to meet their needs.

The final result was an engineering feat that was second to none. Two boxes were hinged together and wheels were attached, They could now fill it up, pack it up and wheel it into a corner. It certainly pleased the Foster Share Shed.

The storage box looked a bit lonely on its own so we threw in a few toys to help with their Xmas appeal.

The natives are getting restless! It has been ten weeks and still no word when the @%#&?* bolt can be fixed to the back door. The boys are getting cabin fever and it is having a depressing effect on them.

Members are asking "what are the committee doing to solve the problem?" All we can say is that we have bent over backwards to co-operate with the college but the wheels of the Education Department tend to turn at their own pace. Our fingers are well and truly crossed for a result soon.

To show our thanks to David Templeman for the support he has given us over the past twenty years we issued a Certificate of Appreciation acknowledging his great work in keeping us going.. His efforts have helped men to carry out some usefulness in their twilight years.

Myself as Secretary, and Allan Lewis as Chairman, visited David at his offices and presented him with the certificate.

Kevin, David Templeman and Allan

As mentioned earlier our major fund raiser at the Children's Festival was cancelled this year, so it was opportune for us to be invited to set up a stall at the annual Wellness Wednesday event held on the Mandurah foreshore.

We loaded up the new trailer and off we went to set up for business. Our good friends Bunnings helped out by donating a gazebo to annex to the trailer and some fold up trestles to display the toys for sale. The interest shown with our toys was really pleasing and sales were excellent. Having EFTPOS now was a boon, as there was twice as many EFTPOS sales than cash.

Ready for business

YEAR 2020

As we were heading towards Xmas, a number of grannies asked for the address of the Shed so they could come and have a look at what we have available. There is no doubt that grannies are one of our best "target markets". Who best to spoil the grandkids?

The Serpentine/Jarrahdale Shire conduct an annual Community Fair which culminates in a log chop competition. It attracts a huge crowd, but unfortunately this year it fell victim to COVID 19 and was cancelled. The Serpentine/Jarrahdale Men's Shed decided to organise a community markets event to take its place and invited other Sheds to participate.

There were four Sheds, including us, that participated, together with a spattering of local businesses and community groups. We felt that it might be an opportunity to boost our sales, so we loaded up the new trailer and off we went.

We were not disappointed. Although the number of people attending was only around 650, the interest in our goodies was fantastic. It seemed that most families had children and the wooden toys were like a magnet to them. It was not only a heap of toys that people bought, but the kid's furniture was in demand. Some people put in orders for items for Xmas.

The Serpentine/Jarrahdale Men's Shed told us that even if the usual Fair is run next year by the Shire, they will organise another Community Shed Day at a different time. That event will definitely be put in the diary for next year.

Allen, Allan, Phil, Norm and Kevin ready for customers

CHAPTER 43

In early December the City of Mandurah conducted what they called "Christmas Week". There were Christmas Lights Trail, street level performers, children's activities and entertainment on different nights of the week.

Community groups were invited to promote their operation and we were asked to show what goodies we produce at the Men's Shed. We must be special because they allocated us the prime position of the rotunda for the Thursday night.

Rather than sell our toys, we decided that the Men's Shed would provide a selection of small, wheeled toys free of charge to the kids who attended on the night.

As the 2020 Children's Festival had been cancelled this was an opportunity to provide these toys we would normally give out at the Festival.

We usually have the children glue the wheels on, but COVID 19 restrictions dictated that we have as little physical contact with the children as possible.

It was an interesting night as most families were just out for a casual stroll on a balmy summer's night. There was only a spattering of community group displays so people weren't treating it as a look and see night. Because of this families just had eyes front and not giving us a second glance.

We had toys to give away, so we couldn't have that. Out I went as a spruiker and told everyone who came along with children that we were giving away free toys. It is amazing how many people were sceptical that we had "free toys". In fact I had to earnestly convince some parents it was so. Short of me dragging them in, they tentatively climbed the steps to the rotunda but they soon found out it was the case.

We were surprised that there were not more people out as the night had been well advertised as a "Christmas Lights Trail" for children. Still, all was not lost as we managed to give away about 200 toys on the night. This was far from what we had planned

YEAR 2020

Kevin, Peter, Allan, Bob and David get toys ready

for the night, but as it was our first time at an event like this we chalked it up to experience.

People are very supportive knowing we are a not-for-profit operation that supports community groups. Although we assured the parents and grannies that the toys were free, we received $240 in donations on the night.

As there were still some 400 toys left it was decided to continue the free give-a-ways at the Mandjar Markets which operate on a Sunday on the eastern foreshore.

Setting up shop at the Mandjar Markets proved to be a good move for us. Despite being washed out just after lunch, there was a steady stream of business all morning. It is interesting to see how the dynamics of toy buying at these type of events changes from time to time. Usually "grannies" make up around 70% of our sales. This time it was only about 55%. Am not sure what this means, but it did not affect our overall sales. Our takings on the day were as good as any event at which we have attended. Being close to Xmas, we took a chance on being at the markets, which turned out to be a good decision.

The stallholder numbers were down due to COVID 19 business closures but the public were still there on the day. We may have even had a better result if the markets had not been shut down due to inclement weather after lunch. Ah well, you can't win them all.

In addition to our sales, we also managed to give away another 230 small toys. Guess what? Another $300 in donations! Aren't people wonderful?

Despite our reduced attendance hours and less attendees, those who do come to the Shed are doing a great job continuing to produce toys and kiddie furniture. It is a credit to these guys that they box on with an attitude of *"In the face of adversity, we shall succeed".* Half of them were around when that statement was originally coined.

This typifies what our "Shed Men" are all about. It is selfless time they put in to produce with pride, something that will bring a smile to a young face. It is not a task to them; it is more a privilege to be able to work beside likeminded people and enjoy some fellowship.

Here we are just a few days before we shut down for the Xmas break and winding up another year.. The boys are battling on to make sure a few special orders are completed on time. This happens every year as parents and grannies rush in at the last moment wanting to provide a Xmas present for the kids. Does this worry us? Not in the slightest. It is all part of what we are about.

Despite the long break we had due to COVID 19 we still managed to get some toys out to groups;

- Child and Parent Centre Dudley Park
- Embrace@Telethon Kids Institute
- Mandurah Arts and Crafts
- Seascapes Community Group
- Goodstart Early Learning Meadow Springs
- Foster Share Shed
- Rotary Club Mandurah Districts
- Wearne House
- Tiny House Mandurah

The Shed is closed and the gates are locked as another year ends for us. It has been an "interesting" year as we have had to face some trying times.

The COVID 19 situation had a profound effect on operations as we saw the Shed closed for a few months. This affected our members as they found themselves denied access to their break away from home.

The change in College policies also had members restricted to times when students were not in school. There is light at the end of the tunnel through as the college is implementing changes so that in the new year we can attend while students are in class.

Apart from the access door to the school grounds being bolted, additional signage has to be installed in relation to fire emergency exits. A new egress door has to be installed in our back room and both rooms furnished with additional fire extinguishers.

All of this is in the name of "safety". As most of these changes are for the benefit of the Shed most of the cost has to be borne by us. We hate to guess what that cost will be, but if it means we can continue on then we will have to grin and bear it.

It will be a much better working environment next year as we see things returning to some sort of normality.

Due to the lateness in the day that we could be at the college, it was agreed that our usual wind up BBQ would not be held. It was considered that the numbers would not be there.

Instead, there is to be a Saturday luncheon at a local café at which partners can also attend. There was to be no cost subsidy by the Shed as it was considered not to be appropriate.

As this year is the end of two decades of Shed operations I thought I would show in the following pages some of the marvellous toys that have brought the smiles to children's faces. It is not all of them but it is a pretty good representation.

FROM TOY BOYS TO SHED MEN

YEAR 2020

JOURNEY'S END

Well, that's it folks. The end of a two decade journey that started with a humble beginning in a backyard shed and grew to become a forty member operation that has developed into a respected reputation within the community of Mandurah.

Not only is it a place where men can share some camaraderie, put their skills to good use and give something back to the community but find comfort in having peace of mind in a caring environment.

While making toys is a major part of what we do, helping people out with minor jobs or repairs and completing special projects for community groups forms a wonderful part of our overall operation.

When I first started this project my idea was that I would list out the people who have worked at the shed over the years and jot down a few anecdotes of things that have happened. This could be then rolled out in to a few pages and a copy given to each member.

However, as I delved into the records I found that there was a lot more to the journey than I realised. Just like Norman Lindsay's Magic Pudding, just when I thought I had come to an end, up popped something else to keep things going.

Would you believe it? The following email actually came in as I was writing this piece:

> Hi Guys
> We went to the foreshore and were surprised with a free toy for my Grandson, He picked a little dog.
> I would just like you to know that's little dog goes everywhere with him, he sleeps with it every night. The little dog even has a bath. My Grandson has had a hard year but this little dog has brought a smile to his face.
> I would like to Thank everyone at the Men's shed, especially the man who

made the little dog. THANK YOU..

Merry Christmas
Kim

There are so many stories like this that I would be writing for the next twenty years if I tried to cover them all. People are constantly surprised to learn what we produce is so lovingly made in such a basic way. I think it is the simplicity of our toys that has the attraction.

This is why our guys love to make children's wooden toys.

Where to from here? As having premises to operate from has been a stumbling block over the years, the feeling in the group is that we should now be seriously investigating securing our own premises. The members want to have peace of mind in knowing they can control their own destiny, particularly in deciding what hours we can open.

We are very spoilt with the conditions of tenure at the college, but we are not in control of working times. There is always the possibility that the college will need to "repossess" their rooms some time in the future and we will have to move anyway. The college has actually commented that it is a strong possibility the college will be redeveloped in ten years or so.

The best scenario is to have a block of land provided to us by the City of Mandurah and then design a building that will suit for many years to come. It may be that a new Shed will not only be able to cater for woodworking, but maybe a metal working operation and an area were members can come for just a cuppa and a chat with others.

Many Sheds throughout WA cater for those who just want a social outlet. I am not sure if it is because other areas do not have a Senior Citizens Centre, but it works well for them.

It won't happen overnight, but I am sure it will happen.

It has been just the best experience for me to be able to not only learn how the Shed has developed, but given me a great sense of pride to know that I have been able to document this journey. I still have plans to somehow provide each member with a copy. My fingers are crossed that I can get this published, but if not the answer might be to download it onto USBs. Despite many of the older guys being technically challenged, they should be able to find a relative or friend who has a computer or laptop to provide the answer.

This may be "Journey's End" but it is far from the end of the Mandurah Men's Shed. I would like to see the next twenty years of operations documented in a similar manner. There is no way I will be at the Shed for the next twenty years, so I hope successors keep the records going. Those people can change the title or the format, but I do hope they keep the ball rolling.

You may recall that I told you how the Shed was open Tuesday to Friday and members allocated one or two days to attend. Because of our numbers, this was to give a fair go for all to be able to attend. As a result we usually had different faces on each day.

To sign off I have put my twist on the old poem "Monday's child is ....". I think it sums up our Shed.

Tuesday's Men are aged of face.

Wednesday's Men still have some grace.

Thursday's Men have known some woe.

Friday's Men aren't far to go.

......AND ALTOGETHER THEY ARE LOVING AND GIVING

THE AUTHOR

Kevin Atkins was born in 1942 and raised in Perth.

His working life entailed office positions but he developed a liking for woodworking at high school. His father was responsible for teaching him the finer points of woodworking, together with the identification and use of the various tools.
It was a natural progression therefore that when he retired he would seek out a Men's Shed.

"Writing this journey is my way of saying "Thank You" to the Mandurah Men's Shed for the pleasure it has given me"

Kim's Toyboys

MANDURAH MEN'S SHED